# The Young Maestros

Thelma Manning

## Contents



Oxford University Press
Music Department, Walton Street, Oxford OX2 6DP

*Oxford University Press, Walton Street, Oxford OX2 6DP*

*Oxford New York Toronto*
*Delhi Bombay Calcutta Madras Karachi*
*Kuala Lumpur Singapore Hong Kong Tokyo*
*Nairobi Dar es Salaam Cape Town*
*Melbourne Auckland*

*and associated companies in*
*Beirut Berlin Ibadan Nicosia*

OXFORD *is a trade mark of Oxford University Press*



*First published 1986*
*ISBN 0 19 321424 5*

*Designed by Ann Samuel*
*Illustrated by Annabel Large and Mark Peppé*

*Typeset by Oxford Publishing Services, Oxford*
*Printed in Hong Kong*

## Acknowledgements

The author and publishers are grateful to the following for permission to include their copyright photographs:
p. 5 A. F. Brown; pp. 13, 21, 54, 75 BBC Hulton Picture Library.

The author wishes to thank Miss M. C. Jones for valuable experience gained while teaching under her headship at Larchfield School.

## Note to the teacher

*The Young Maestros* offers a fresh and practical approach to an aspect of music that in recent times has been neglected in primary schools.

It contains stories about incidents in the lives of eight famous composers when they were young, followed by musical activities, including listening, playing and creative work. Each section has simple background information on the composer and his music, plus questions, vocabulary work and non-musical activities.

*The Young Maestros* has something to offer both the music specialist and the class teacher, who will find much of the material usable in the context of his/her day to day class work in language and other subjects.

The sign **1 ♫** indicates that there is a piano arrangement of a particular piece of music at the back of the book.

**Handel**

# Music at Midnight

Have you ever done anything exciting in the middle of the night, when everyone else was asleep? Have you ever had a pillow-fight, or a midnight feast? Well, if you have, you'll know just how the boy in this story felt . . .

George Handel could hardly wait! He had discovered an old clavichord (an instrument rather like a small piano) and, with the help of some of the grown-up members of the family, had managed to smuggle it into an attic room at the top of the house.

It had all been done very quietly, so as not to annoy George's father, who was not at all happy about George learning music.

But George had it all planned! He intended creeping up to the attic every night, when everyone else was asleep, so that he could try to play some tunes on the clavichord.

He sat up in bed, and listened to the clock striking—nine, ten, eleven—and at last he heard twelve strokes. The time had come! It was midnight!

He got up, and, opening the bedroom door very quietly, crept step by step up the stairs which led to the attic—being very careful not to make any of them squeak!

He reached the attic and looked joyfully at the clavichord. George loved music (although he couldn't tell you why!) and at last he was near to the very thing which could make tunes! George gently touched the keys, and, little by little, his fingers worked out some of the pieces which he knew.

He forgot all about the cold and dark attic room (lit only by the one candle which George had carried with him so that he could see). In fact, he forgot everything except his pleasure in working out tunes to play.

George went up to the attic room night after night—until at last he had managed to work out how to play his *favourite tune*! He grew so excited that he began to play loudly—then even more loudly, until . . . what do you think? The door burst open, and in walked George's father, who had been disturbed by the music.

'No more music for you, my lad,' he roared. 'Back to bed—at once!' George needed no second bidding and went off without saying one single word!

It was a long time before George was allowed to play any pieces again, but he never stopped wanting to become a musician. He grew up to be a famous composer in spite of everything, and never forgot about the time he made music at midnight.

## Words to remember

**Composer** A person who makes up his or her own music.

## Musical names to remember

**Clavichord** A fairly small keyboard instrument, which is rather like a mini piano.

**Keys** The separate parts of a keyboard, on such instruments as the *piano* or *clavichord*, which are pressed or moved down individually, in order to make the sound.

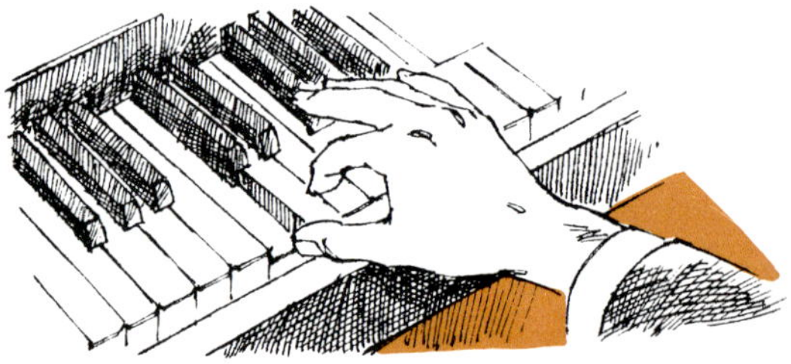

**March** A brisk tune used by soldiers on parade, who have to keep in time with the music.

**Hornpipe** A dance for sailors.

**Jig** A quick, lively dance.

**Minuet** A rather slow, graceful dance, once used at court balls. It was very popular with kings, queens, and other important people.

**Opera** A story which is set to music and sung and acted on a stage by one or two men and women (called soloists) and by a larger group of people (called the chorus).

You will see some of these names when you look at *Music to use*.

## Things to learn

George Frideric Handel was born in Halle, Germany. When Handel grew up, he was eager to learn more about music, so he went to Italy to listen to the music performed there, especially Italian opera. Later, he visited England, and was pleased to hear the first performance of his *own* opera, called *Rinaldo*. In fact, his visit to this country was so successful, that, after going back to Germany for a while, Handel returned to England, where he settled for the rest of his life.

Handel wrote operas; but, like the popular music of today, fashions change, and people like to hear new styles. So when the public seemed to be growing tired of opera, Handel decided to write religious music—but still for people to sing. He chose bible tales as ideas for some of these 'singing stories', and he became so wrapped up in his composing that he even forgot to eat!

These religious stories set to music were sung (but, unlike opera, not acted) and were called **oratorios**. The most famous of Handel's oratorios is called *Messiah*, which is another way of saying Saviour, and is another name given to Jesus Christ.

## Musical activities

**1** Here is a rhythm pattern:

Clap or tap this pattern several times after it has been played to you by your teacher.

Some people think that Handel, who made up this pattern, had these words in mind when he wrote this tune: 'Please be kind to me'. 'Please be kind to me'.

Now say these words as you clap the rhythm pattern, like this:

Please be kind to me — and so on.

Now listen to a recording of the music all the way through and try to spot the pattern

whenever it comes. The tune is printed below for you to follow.

**Air** from *The Water Music* suite by Handel

Finally, count how many times the pattern comes throughout the whole of the piece.

You may like to know that this piece is called an *Air* and comes from the famous *Water Music* suite by Handel. (See *Music to Use* p. 93 for details of piano arrangements.)

**2** Here is a famous tune by Handel from one of his oratorios, *Judas Maccabaeus*.

You will see that it only uses five different notes G A B C D.

If you know these five notes on your recorder

a) Play them one after the other: G A B C D
b) Then play them the other way round: D C B A G
c) Now play B C D
d) Now practise the 'jump'—D–G
e) Now try to play the tune above.

You have now heard, or played, a complete **phrase**, or musical sentence. Here is the 'answering sentence':

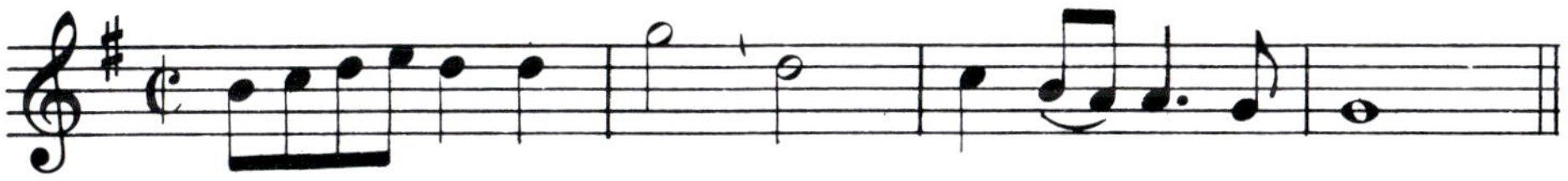

If you can't yet play all of these notes on your recorder, ask your teacher to play this phrase. It is rather like asking a question, which is answered by the teacher. Now repeat the whole 'musical game', as follows:

Now listen to the complete piece. Your tune comes at the opening, and is repeated several times. Get ready to play your tune whenever it comes.

## Questions to answer

1 Where was George Handel born?
2 What instrument did George play, in order to teach himself his favourite tunes?
3 Why did George practise in the attic in the middle of the night?
4 Did George's father manage to stop George's growing love of music?
5 Which country did George finally settle in, when he grew up?
6 What was the name of George Handel's most famous religious work or *oratorio?*

## Things to do

1 Look in your school or local library, or in any record department or music shop, and try to find out the names of any other pieces by Handel. Remember that record-covers are not only nice to look at, but also very useful!
2 Draw a picture showing a scene from a part of this story. Perhaps you could show George Handel creeping up the stairs in his night-shirt, with a candle in his hand.
3 Pretend that *you* are George Handel, and that you are writing to your best friend (who has recently moved) to tell him how mean your father is, because he won't let you learn music. You *know* that you can trust your friend, so write freely and tell him exactly how you feel about this.
4 Act a scene from this story for an assembly about 'Famous People'. Perhaps you could do the 'attic scene' where George is discovered by his father.

Bach

# Sebastian's Secret

Have you ever done anything in secret? Have you ever had a tree-house, or a special part of the garden, or a hide-out near the river's edge, or a corner of a shed where you had private meetings with a group of friends, without the grown-ups knowing?

Well, if you have, you'll know just how the boy in this story felt.

Johann Sebastian could hardly keep his eyes open! His eldest brother, Johann Christoph, was quite surprised, for Sebastian wasn't usually lazy or dozy.

Eleven-year-old Johann Sebastian Bach was an orphan, as both his parents had died. So he and his older brother, Jacob, lived with his grown-up brother, Christoph, who took charge of his younger brothers, and helped Sebastian with his music lessons.

'Play the piece I asked you to learn a few days ago,' cried Johann Christoph. 'Mm . . . remarkably good, Sebastian, you played that well, in spite of your tired eyes and constant yawning.'

Sebastian put his hand to his mouth and tried to stifle another big yawn. He loved his music lessons, but today he felt almost too tired to answer. His big brother continued: 'Why! What is the matter with you, boy? Wake up!'

'I'm alright, really,' began Sebastian. 'Do let me play . . .'

'Enough!' interrupted his big brother sharply, 'I haven't time for drowsy pupils!'

Johann Christoph, although wanting to do his best, wasn't always very patient, for he was not a rich man, and often found it hard enough to keep his own young family, without caring for his two younger brothers as well.

'I know all the pieces you have given me to learn—please

let me use the wonderful music in the big book which you have locked away in the cupboard. I tried to copy a tune the other day, but the candle went out, and . . .'

'What?' interrupted Sebastian's big brother, yet again, 'Wasting candles to look at my most treasured possession? Whatever next!'

'Please let me see it—please, *please*,' begged Sebastian.

'No,' retorted Christoph, 'not yet, you're too young.'

'*Please*!' begged Sebastian, again.

'I said—No! That's enough!' replied his brother, even more sharply. 'My book is not for you!'

So that, you might think, was that!

But, of course, having already tired himself out by trying to get hold of the book, one night when no-one else was about, Sebastian wasn't going to give up that easily. After a long, long time, he thought he'd found a way of reaching the music . . . and he certainly wasn't the kind of boy who would readily take 'no' for an answer!

So every time the moon shone brightly enough for Sebastian to see, he would creep out of bed in the middle of the night while the rest of the family were asleep, and go to his brother's big book containing the music of various composers.

Night after night, Sebastian stayed awake, waiting for the household to sleep. Then, as soon as all was quiet, he would creep down—bare-footed, so as not to wake the baby (who, as you can imagine, would be sure to cry if disturbed, and spoil the whole plan!).

The moon shone on the lattice door of the cupboard, so that Sebastian could see to copy out the different pieces.

Shh! What was that? A creak, as somebody stirred in his sleep; a snore from big brother, Christoph; the rustle of leaves outside . . . Sebastian hardly dared to breathe! Yet no-one woke; so he went on copying as quickly as he could, forgetting all about the time passing by, or about how tired he would feel when he had to go to school, early next morning. Sebastian was so clever at music that he could sometimes hear the tunes in his mind as he copied them.

'What fantastic tunes,' he murmured to himself, as he

wrote, 'I *must* copy all of them. I'll be alright as long as Christoph doesn't find out what I'm doing.'

He strained his eyes to read the music and wrote as fast as he could without leaving out a single note. The clock struck one, two, three, four . . . He must stop soon, in case his brothers woke early and found that he was not in bed. His quill pen raced over the manuscript as fast as he could move it . . .

As time went on, and Sebastian's great secret remained undiscovered, he became rather more daring. Feeling that he had kept his secret well, he started to try out some of the music which he had copied on his brother's clavichord. This (as you'll remember if you have heard the Handel story) was a quiet keyboard instrument not generally likely to disturb others when played.

Just like the young George Handel, Sebastian grew more and more excited at the lovely sounds which this new music made. Gradually, he became so absorbed that he forgot about everything else until . . . well, you know, I expect, what is coming next . . . finally, his big brother overheard and burst into the room.

'You are not playing one of the pieces which I gave you to practise,' he cried. 'Where did you get that music?'

Sebastian was too startled at being caught to reply.

'Show me, boy!' roared his brother. 'When I think of all I have done for you—taking you into my home, helping you with your music, giving you pieces to learn—and what do you do to repay me? You copy from my own special book, you disobey me, you stay awake at night when you should be asleep. Shame—shame on you!'

Sebastian still did not utter a word, standing still as though rooted to thc spot!

'You wicked boy!' went on his brother, 'using music from my very own book. Why—you're no better than a thief!' And so saying, Johann Christoph roughly snatched the music which it had taken Sebastian six months to copy!

'I'm not—I'm not!' cried Johann Sebastian, by now too angry to be very frightened. 'I didn't *steal* the music, I just *copied* it. *I'm* no thief!'

Do you know, before his astonished brother had time to reprimand him again, Sebastian turned away, declaring as he left the room: 'Anyway, I know most of the music from memory, now, after all that time spent in copying. So it doesn't matter what you say, or do, any more, because this music is in my head—*SO THERE*!'

Needless to add, Sebastian did not stay to hear his brother's reply! And he never went to the book cupboard again.

But I'm pleased to tell you that the two brothers patched up their quarrel and did 'make it up.'

You know, Sebastian never did forget that music. And I expect that it gave him some useful ideas when he himself grew up to be one of the greatest composers which the world has ever known.

So, you see, Sebastian's secret wasn't wasted, after all!

## Words to remember

**Constant** To go on repeatedly.

**Treasured possession** Something dearly loved by the owner.

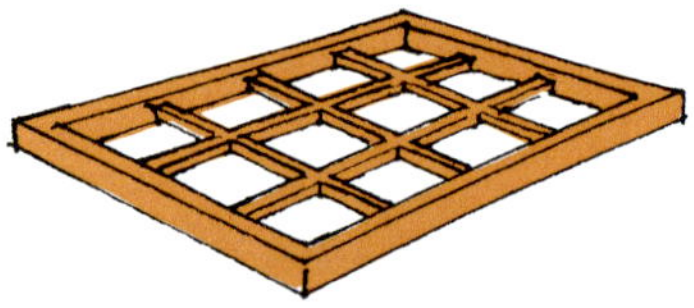

**Lattice** Wooden, wire or metal strips which make squares across a frame.

**Note** The sign which shows each musical sound.

**Quill pen** The sharp, pointed end of the feather of a fairly large bird, used as a pen.

**Manuscript** Paper especially made for writing music.

**Reprimand** To show someone that you are very cross!

## Things to learn

St Thomas's Church, Leipzig, where Bach was director of music for most of his life.

Bach was born in Eisenach, Germany. In some ways he was a kind of music explorer, and liked to find out different ways of making a musical ending to his **chorale** melodies, which are really like **hymn tunes.**

He also explored ways of writing for keyboard instruments, such as the **clavichord** or **organ** (an instrument which has two, or more keyboards) and he composed a set of 48 very famous pieces called *Preludes and Fugues.*

A **prelude** is a piece which always comes at the beginning and leads into another musical piece.

A **fugue** is rather like a musical jigsaw, in which all the pieces, or parts, fit in together to make up a complete musical design, or picture.

Bach was fond of his family and liked to encourage his relations to make music. He wrote some attractive, short keyboard pieces for his second wife; this album is called *The Little Note-book for Anna Magdalena Bach.*

He also helped his sons to learn music by writing pieces for the keyboard. These were like musical studies, and were meant to teach them to play skilfully and well. They were called *Two-Part Inventions.*

An **invention** is a piece which has all kinds of interesting musical ideas.

# Musical activities

1 Some time ago, some amusing words were fitted to the main tunes of Bach's fugues, just for fun. Here are the words to one of these 'Fugue tunes', 'I AM SO HUNGRY'.

Now here is the *tune* which fits these words:

Now here are the words and tune together:

The words and tune come four times at the beginning of this fugue. Perhaps your teacher will play this opening part—slowly—to see if you can fit in the words 'I am so hungry', each time they come, either higher, or lower.

**Fugue in G minor** by Bach
(simplified opening by T. Manning)

1 ♫

2 Here is a tune written by Johann Sebastian Bach. It is called a **musette**, and it is imitating the kind of country piece which might have been played on small bagpipes. It has the *same note*—G—going all the way through, in the underneath part. As it is a quiet, peaceful tune, it could very easily be played by 'bell-like' percussion instruments, such as:

Chime–bars
Glockenspiels
Indian bells
Sleigh bells
Triangles

**Musette** by Bach

Try to group these instruments together and play the piece through with the piano. Make it as pretty as you can.

If you are lucky enough to have a metallophone, or any similar percussion instrument, perhaps a group could play the low G all the way through, to copy the kind of repeated sound which you hear on bagpipes.

## Questions to answer

1 Who took care of Johann Sebastian after his mother and father had died?
2 What was 'Sebastian's secret'?
3 George Frideric Handel (another boy in this book) was born in the same year as Johann Sebastian Bach. In certain parts of their stories they behaved much in the same way. What did they both do?
4 What did Sebastian use to write with?
   **a** fountain pen  **c** quill pen
   **b** biro  **d** felt tip pen
5 What kind of lighting did the Bach family use?
   **a** gas light  **c** candle light
   **b** oil lamps  **d** electric light
6 Where was Sebastian born?

## Things to do

1 Write a short story about Sebastian Bach. Pretend that you are Sebastian, and that you are telling your best school friend (who is the only other person in the whole world to know about you getting up at night) that you have a special secret! No one else is to know about this.
2 Make up three short 'word-phrases' of your own to fit the tune of Bach's fugue, instead of: 'I am so hungry'. For example, you could put:
   **a** 'I'm glad it's snowing' or: **b** 'I do like swimming'.
   Don't write these as two of your word-phrases, though. Use your *own* ideas!
3 Draw a picture of Sebastian copying the music by moonlight.
4 With a group of friends, act a scene from this story. The most exciting part is where Sebastian's brother finds out his secret and is very angry indeed!

**Haydn**

# The Little Drummer

Franz Joseph Haydn sat quite still in a corner of the room, while the grown-ups were talking. He was listening intently to every word which was being said, and he was just longing to join in; but he decided that if he wanted to get his own way, it would be wiser not to interrupt!

'What are we going to do?', asked one of the townsmen.

'All that music without a drummer!' said another man. 'Terrible!'

'Without our drummer to play with the band, we are lost!' cried Cousin Franck, the school and choirmaster with whose family Joseph was living.

Little Joseph, who was only six, could bear it no longer. He just had to speak! 'I could play the drum,' he cried. 'Please let me try, please!'

Everyone was very surprised, and the group of people looked in astonishment at the small, rather grubby little boy, who had until now been sitting so quietly that some of the grown-ups hadn't even noticed that he was there!

'Well', began one person, doubtfully, 'you're not very old . . .'

'You're very small,' began another man.

'Now, look here, young man,' the third person started to say.

'Please!' repeated Joseph. 'I'm nearly seven!'

Cousin Franck, the choirmaster, looked thoughtfully at his little relative, who was nicknamed Sepperl. He knew that Joseph was already becoming very clever at music, and was a really lovely singer.

'You know', he said to the others, 'I do believe that Sepperl might just manage it. There's no harm in showing the lad what to do—I'll give him a try'.

Little Joseph went as red as a beetroot! He ran to the

kitchen before anyone had a chance to disagree with Cousin Franck, and found a flour barrel. He tied a cloth around the top of it, and, with the help of two sticks, began to beat out the rhythm of the music which he had heard the town band practising:

*BOOM! BOOM! BOOM, boom–boom–BOOM!*
*BOOM! BOOM! BOOM, boom–boom–BOOM!*

*PRR! RUM–POM–POM*
*PRR! RUM–POM–POM*

*Pom–Pom–POM POM POM!*
*Pom–Pom–POM POM POM!*

Joseph was completely carried away, and didn't even notice that the flour was escaping from the flour bin and forming a cloud of dust all over everything.

'What a mess!', cried Cousin Franck's wife. 'You naughty boy, Sepperl—you don't deserve to play anywhere! Off to bed.'

Joseph cried all night, and was determined to get up especially early the next morning, to help in the kitchen before school. Then perhaps the grown-ups would let him play the drum.

Luckily, Cousin Franck had noticed how nicely Joseph kept in time with the music.

'Let Sepperl have another try,' he said to his wife the next day. 'I'll show him what to do somewhere else, so that he won't get in your way.'

So Joseph practised every single piece, and watched Cousin Franck all the time, so that he knew exactly how to fit his drum-beat in with the music.

The great moment came, and it was time to start.

The town band and the choir were making music for a special occasion in Hainburg, Austria, where Joseph lived. On each day of the week, the musicians would be singing and playing at a different church, or at a special holy place; or they might be celebrating the festival by grandly parading through the town to the outlying fields.

Joseph stood up in his place smartly, like a soldier, but still he was so small that a hunchback had to carry the drum

fastened to his back while Joseph walked closely just behind, in order to beat time on it with his two drumsticks.

At first, the crowds must have found this a very amusing sight; and I expect that the grown-ups smiled and the young ones giggled when they saw the little drummer following the hunchback with the big drum. But Joseph was so wrapped up in his music that he just didn't notice anything or anybody!

*Bim, bam, BOOM! Bim, bam, BOOM!* went the drum, as Joseph and the hunchback and the other musicians followed the important people such as the mayor and the priest in the procession.

No-one wanted to miss this event, so everyone was watching and listening.

How grand Joseph felt, with his wig and his best clothes on! Now he had become a real musician!

After a while the crowds began to notice how cleverly Joseph kept in time with the music, and how earnestly and skilfully he played. Soon people stopped smiling and, instead, began to say:

'Such a good beat coming from such a little boy!'

'How well he plays!'

'What a nice, crisp sound he makes . . .'

Then a voice amongst the crowd nearest to the musicians called 'Bravo! Bravo!'

'Well done, little Joseph!' called another.

Yet another voice cried, 'Well played!'

And then came the final compliment, 'Salute the young maestro!'

From that moment onwards, Joseph was quite determined to become a musician. When he was only eight, he went to a very famous choir school in Vienna to learn more about music. When he grew up, he became a very good and well loved composer. He never forgot that he had once been a 'star drummer', and that is why you can often hear special parts for the drum in his compositions.

So, if ever *you* get the chance to take part in a musical event, have a try! It might lead to great things!

## Words to remember

**Intently** Thinking earnestly about a particular thing.

**Festival** An important occasion or a celebration to remember a special event, probably with music, singing, dancing and so on.

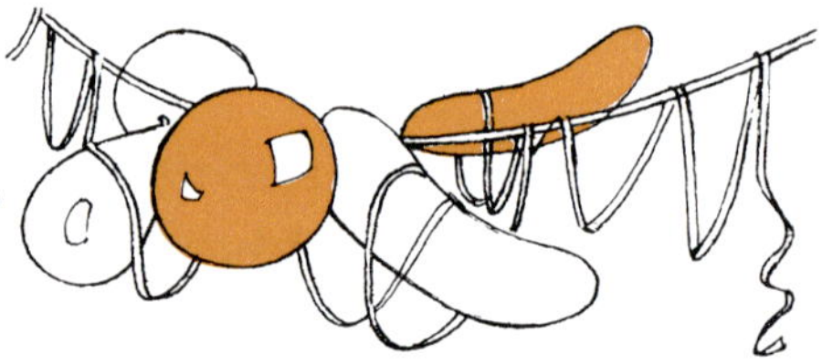

**Parading** Walking, making music, marching in a public procession.

**Skilfully** Neatly and cleverly.

**Compliment** Praise: a way of showing that something is liked.

## Things to learn

Haydn never forgot that he had once been a 'child-star' drummer. You can still see this drum today, if you are lucky enough, in the church at Hainburg. When he became a composer, he wrote some special parts for the drum in some of his famous pieces.

Haydn's school, The Vienna Boys' Choir School, is still very famous today. Sometimes, members of the Choir travel to other countries to sing to people. Perhaps you heard all about this Choir School on the T.V. programme *Blue Peter*?

Some members of the Vienna Boys' Choir School, where Haydn was a pupil, performing in costume.

Haydn liked practical jokes, and sometimes he got into trouble for playing tricks when he was at school. When he grew up, he still liked a joke. In one famous symphony, he made the musicians play an unexpectedly loud sound, after all the soft sounds, just to give everyone a surprise and make them jump. This symphony is generally known as the 'Surprise'.

Once, when Haydn and his **orchestra** (a large group of instrumentalists) were working for a rich nobleman, away from their homes, Haydn wanted everyone to have a chance to visit family and friends.

So he wrote a special **movement** (or part of a piece) making each group of players finish the music one by one, leaving the other musicians when they had finished their parts, and blowing out their nightly candles as they went away. By the end of the piece, it was quite dark and there was hardly anyone left to play!

Luckily, the man for whom Haydn worked just laughed, and said that all the members of the orchestra could have a holiday. This piece is part of a symphony which has since become very famous. It is called the 'Farewell Symphony'. ('Farewell' is another way of saying 'Goodbye'.)

Some of Haydn's other symphonies are also known by special names, such as:

The London Symphony
The Clock Symphony
The Military Symphony
The Toy Symphony.

Haydn was kind and was helpful to younger musicians, so he earned the nickname 'Papa Haydn'.

# Musical activities

2 ♫

**The 'Surprise' Symphony**
by Haydn

1 Here is the opening of the slow movement of Haydn's famous 'Surprise' Symphony. Listen while it is being played.

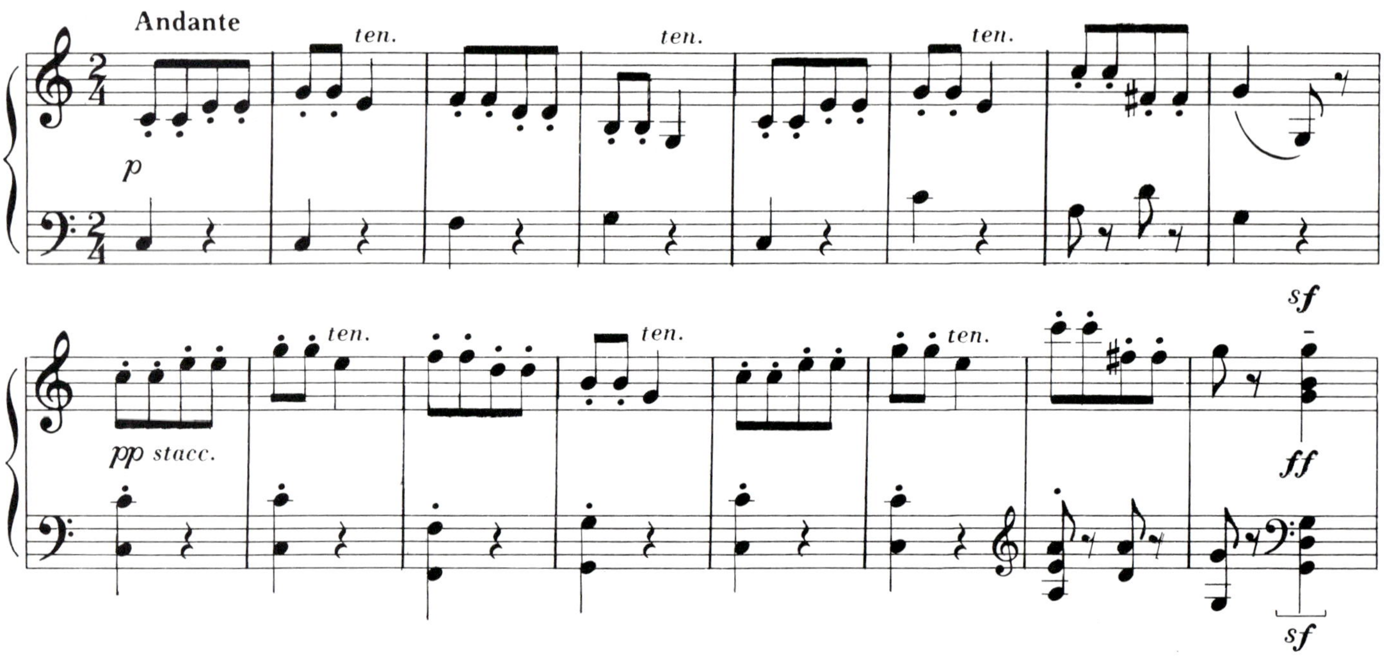

Now listen again and put up your hand when you reach the 'surprise'.

This time, when you hear the music, bang, stamp or clap when you get to the surprise.

Now, add your own percussion parts to this music. The triangles and bells could do the soft, quiet part and the drum and cymbals could play the surprise.

Listen to the next part of this piece which follows the music you have already heard. The complete part is on page 82. If you listen carefully, you will hear two more loud sounds which may come as a surprise.

Now try playing the whole piece, using your percussion instruments. Enjoy the surprises!

3 ♫

2 Here is a Country Dance by Haydn. You will quite often find that country dance music has notes which are

repeated over and over again. Haydn has made his piece sound quite countrified by using the same notes in the underneath piano part.

Listen carefully to this dance. CLAP or TAP the 'OOM–cha–cha' beat.

Here is the left hand part, which is played for the first half of the piece:

Listen again to this dance and try to find out how many times you can hear this little group of notes, or **bar**, altogether.

In the second half of the dance there is a pretty, flowing tune in the top part. Listen very carefully and find out how many times it comes. Don't stop listening, or you might miss hearing it!

Here is the tune which you must listen to:

Perhaps some of you could make up some simple dance steps or movements to go with this dance. Have a try!

3 Haydn liked folk tunes and sometimes you can tell this when you listen to his music. Perhaps these folk tunes came into his mind as he was making up a famous piece, as if to say: 'Now then, Papa Haydn, how about me? I'm a nice little tune you've known for years, so why don't you put *me* into your important piece?'

Here is a long note which you might hear in a Haydn symphony. Count 1–2–3–4 at a fairly fast pace as soon as you hear it:

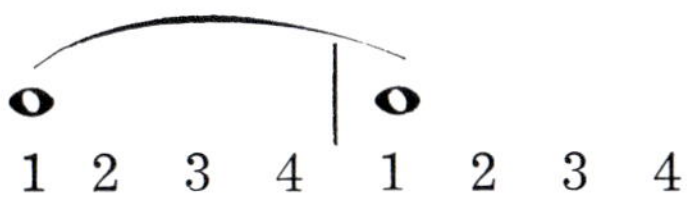


How long does it last? How many beats have you counted altogether?

Now here it is again. How long does it last this time?

When there are a number of repeated bass notes (the same sounds following each other over and over again, in the lowest part of the music) we call this a **ground bass**. You could think of it as rather like a foot being stuck to the ground!

It is said that Haydn might have had a particular folk song in mind while writing one of his symphonies. Here is the tune.

Here are the words of the song.

*Come with me, and you'll be*
*Happy with your days all sunny;*
*And you'll be better thus*
*Than with that old blunderbuss!*
*Oh I know she's got more money,*
*But she doesn't love you, honey;*
*Better thus you will be,*
*Living here so happily.*

(translated by *Elizabeth Fiske*)

⋆ *blunderbuss* — an old-fashioned type of gun. Here means the plain, bad tempered girl friend!

Perhaps you could sing this folk song, or play it on your recorders, chime bars, glockenspiel or xylophones. Some bell-like instruments might just play top D–G all the way through, like this:

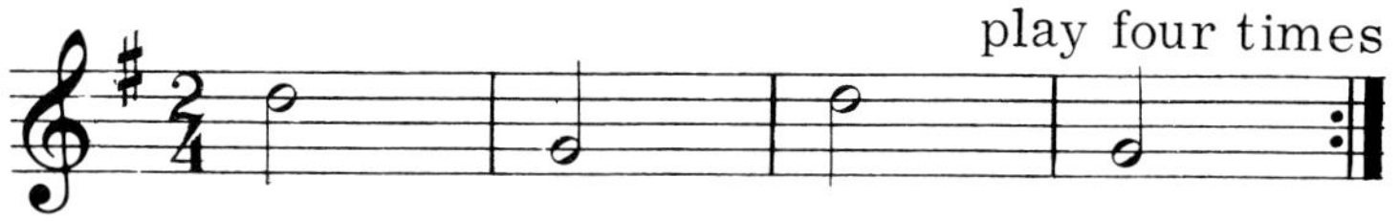


and so on.

You should find that this has a nice, chiming effect.

4 ♫ Here is part of the famous symphony by Haydn. It is called the 'London', because Haydn went to the capital of England to play some of his music, and this symphony was first performed there.

If you listen carefully you might be able to hear how long the held notes in the lower parts last. You may notice that the cheerful tune in the top part of the music is not quite the same as it is in the folk song, but it is still as lively and enjoyable.

Just sit back and have a nice time while listening.

4 When Haydn came to England, he noticed that everyone stood to attention when a special tune was played or sung on important occasions.

'Why is that?' he asked.

'Goodness me! Don't you know?' came the reply. 'We are standing in honour of our national tune, the signature tune which belongs to our country—our National Anthem. We play it when royalty appear, for example.'

5 ♫ Haydn thought this was such a good idea that he decided to write one for the Emperor of Austria as soon as he got home—and he did! You will find this tune on page 84. In this country we use it as a hymn tune, and, if you look at the music, you will find the name of the composer and his country, Austria, written above the tune.

So now you know how this tune came to be written! It is a good, rousing tune, so enjoy singing it!

## Questions to answer

1 In which country did Haydn live?
2 Why did Cousin Franck think that Joseph might be able to play the drum well with the town band?
3 Cousin Franck's wife was cross with Joseph. What had he done to annoy her?
4 Why did the hunchback have to carry the drum for Haydn?
5 Name two important people who walked in front of the town band in the grand procession.
6 Where is Haydn's drum to-day?

## Things to do

1 When Haydn was living, the only way in which people could hear music was by playing it themselves or by going to hear other people performing, often walking miles in order to do so. (Carriages, like taxis today, were expensive to hire; and not everyone had one of his own.) Today people are very lucky, because it is possible to hear music in many different places, and in many different ways. Make a list of all the ways in which we can hear music today.
For example, you could start your list like this:
(a) We can hear music on the radio; and so on.
2 Write down six of Haydn's symphonies which have special names.
3 In the story, it tells you how Haydn invented his own home-made drum. Make some of your own percussion instruments. Here are some suggestions:
**a** An empty washing-up liquid bottle filled with dried peas, beans or loose beads makes a very good rattle.

b Two old saucepan lids of about the same size can make a pair of cymbals.

c Glasses of different sizes, filled with water, and tapped gently, can make some pretty sounds.

d Two rulers—or, better still, two smooth, fairly short and thin pieces of wood—make good rhythm-sticks.

Why not form your *own* band?

Decorate and colour your instruments so that they look like the 'real thing'. No wonder that the percussion part of the orchestra is sometimes nicknamed 'the kitchen'! Have fun!

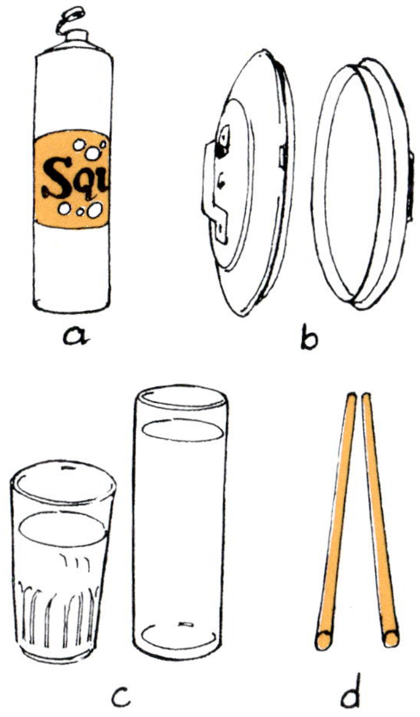


4 When you have got your own band going, perhaps your teacher would help you to find a piece of music in which everybody can stop playing, one by one.

Then you could make up a short play about Haydn and his orchestra working for the rich nobleman, and act the scenes where all the musicians leave one after the other. Don't forget to blow your candle out!

5 In the story, you heard about the celebration and the procession of people: the priest, the mayor, the choir and the town band, with little Joseph closely following the hunchback.

*Either*

a Imagine that you are one of the excited people in the crowd watching this colourful scene. Describe what you saw and heard, and how you felt.

*or*

b Draw or paint a picture of this scene showing the procession, and Joseph and the hunchback.

6 During his visits to England, Haydn went to these three well-known cities: London, Oxford and Cambridge.

a For what reasons are these cities famous?

b Look at a map of England and find out whether these cities are in the Northern or Southern part of the country.

c Now find out which rivers flow through part of these three cities.

Mozart

# Magic Wonder Boy

Have you ever been to Buckingham Palace to see the Queen? If you have, you're very lucky! Here is a story about a boy who visited a royal lady, in a real palace, many years ago.

'Woferl, Woferl—hurry! We can't be late in getting to the palace!' Woferl, whose real name was Wolfgang, quickly appeared in answer to his sister's call, looking splendid in his court costume, which had been given to him by none other than the great Empress of Austria. He wore a lilac coat, and a very fine waistcoat, both of which had a handsome trimming of gold braid. He had a fine cravat with lace at the front, and a smart, powdered wig, tied at the back with a ribbon.

'My!' exclaimed Nannerl, 'you look like a little prince, Master Woferl! What about me? I'm dressed up, too. What do you think of *my* outfit?'

Nannerl was five years older than Wolfgang (who was only six) and pranced in front of her brother, skipping about as much as her costume would allow.

She wore a white, taffeta dress, which had lace trimmings to the sleeve and neckline. Around her neck she had a silky band with a ribbon at the front, and she wore pearl drop earrings and a piece of jewellery in her hair.

'Oh, Nannerl! You do look fine—and so grown up!' said Wolfgang, looking up at his big sister with large, round, admiring eyes.

Nannerl felt pleased to hear his praise, for already she was beginning to understand that Wolfgang was better at music than she was.

Of course, she knew that she could play the harpsichord very well. Papa was always telling her so, and urging her to do more and more practice, and to play even harder pieces.

But Wolfgang could do just anything in music! He could

make up tunes on the spur of the moment; he could at once play even the hardest of pieces given to him by the curious and wondering grown-ups (who didn't often admit that they weren't really as clever as he already was!).

Wolfgang wasn't yet seven; but already he had played (together with Nannerl) before an Elector (or ruler) and his grand household in Munich.

Do you know, the little boy could even play the clavier and balance coins on his hands at the same time!

He had also performed for the rich people in Vienna. One day, an amazed nobleman had said, 'Goodness me! Master Wolfgang is quite a little magician! I can't think of any musical tricks which he *can't* do!'

'Play my tune backwards,' said another admirer—and Wolfgang did.

'Make up another tune like it,' said someone else—and he did.

'Play this tune twice as fast as it is supposed to be played,' called an elaborately dressed lady—and, of course, Wolfgang did!

'Now play it with one finger,' cried yet another person; and Wolfgang did so without any trouble at all.

'Make the tune higher . . . now lower . . .' They went on and on—and each time Wolfgang easily did what they asked him to do.

'Aha! I don't suppose that you could play this difficult piece without taking it home first to practise,' said a grown-up composer (who was becoming rather jealous of such a little boy proving to be so clever). Needless to say, Wolfgang at once played the piece, most beautifully!

'Well, Master Magician', said a proud voice from amongst the audience, 'I shouldn't think that even *you* could play blindfolded, with a handkerchief tied over your eyes . . .' But no one could trick Wolfgang, so of course, although he couldn't see a thing, he still played brilliantly!

Leopold Mozart, Wolfgang's father, was a musician, and he had taught Wolfgang since he was a very small boy. Papa Mozart, having taught his two children a great deal about music, had decided to take his family to Vienna, the

capital of Austria, to show everyone how well his son and daughter played and how clever Wolfgang was.

On the day when the two children were dressed so smartly, the Mozart family—Papa, Mama, Nannerl (whose real name was Marianna) and Wolfgang—were all going to pay another visit to the Empress of Austria; and Nannerl and Wolfgang were going to perform at Schönbrunn, in her grand palace.

They set out in fine style. The driver led the four horses, and the Mozarts settled inside the special coach. How proud Papa Mozart felt to be journeying in such comfort, and to be once more showing off his children to the Royal Family. When they reached the palace, they marvelled yet again at the huge rooms with beautiful, painted ceilings, at the sparkling lights and the rich, colourful hangings.

'This way, please,' said a uniformed steward, who led them to a splendid room in which the two children were to play for their royal audience.

The Empress greeted them kindly; and so did her children, especially Maria Antonia, whom Wolfgang thought was the prettiest little girl he had ever seen!

She, too, could play the clavichord, and she was so friendly when she talked to Wolfgang.

'Let me show you everything,' she said, when the music-making was over. 'I have my own instrument and we have our own, special rooms—and we also have our own park!'

'Come now!' she commanded, kindly, but proudly, for, being the daughter of an Empress, she was like a princess, and well used to giving orders which were at once obeyed.

Wolfgang and Marianne followed the royal children eagerly. Wolfgang was determined not to hold his sister's hand, as he didn't want to seem babyish in front of royalty! But the great, shining floors of the palace were highly polished, and poor Wolfgang slipped and fell.

Maria Antonia, being a kind little girl, went to help him up. So what do you think that Wolfgang did? Well, he actually *kissed* her! Nannerl and the other royal children stood quite still, as though frozen to the spot; for ordinary boys (however clever) just did not kiss the daughter of the

great Empress who ruled over many lands!

But Maria Antonia just smiled; so Wolfgang, encouraged by her kindness, then said, 'One day, I'm going to marry you!'

For a second, nobody said a word. Then Nannerl, wondering what on earth Wolfgang was going to say next, and not wanting to find herself disgraced by her little brother, said, 'Silly boy! Maria Antonia is a *Royal* girl—and you are only an ordinary boy—so how can you talk like that?'

But before Wolfgang could answer, Maria Antonia laughed and said, 'Wolfgang isn't ordinary, he's a magician!' So everyone knew that everything was alright.

Then Wolfgang and Maria Antonia looked at each other, and exchanged a secret smile, as though they already knew that one day they would both become very famous.

You might like to know what really happened when they both grew up.

Maria Antonia, who was called an Arch-Duchess in her own country, didn't marry Wolfgang. Instead, she married the man who became King of France, and the French people called her Queen Marie-Antoinette.

Wolfgang didn't marry any princess or rich lady. However, although he was at times very poor, and rather lonely, he never gave up writing and playing the most beautiful music. He wrote so many great pieces, that, in a way, he did become a king—a king of music. He also wrote some famous operas, and his last one, *The Magic Flute*, was based on a kind of fairy story. So, even when he was quite grown up, I don't think he ever really stopped being a magician, do you?

## Words to remember

**Court** The palace or stately home where the King and Queen live, attended by grand lords and ladies.

**Empress** A royal lady who is rather like a queen, but who is ruler of several countries instead of just one.

**Braid** Narrow ribbon, or tape, used for trimming clothes.

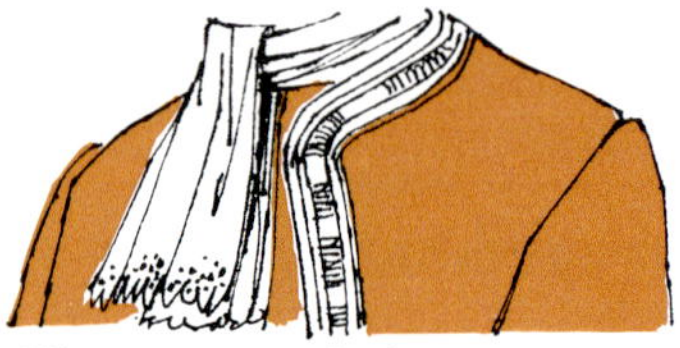

**Cravat** A lightweight scarf which went around the neck and was tied at the front smartly.

**Taffeta** A glossy, lightweight, silky material suitable for a party dress.

**Steward** A person who waits on other people.

**Capital** The main, most important city in the country.

## Musical names to remember

**Harpsichord** An instrument rather like a grand piano which generally has two keyboards. It has a rather 'twangy' sound.

**Clavier** In the time of Mozart, any keyboard instrument such as the clavichord or harpsichord.

## Things to learn

### Entertainments

You have just heard about the kind of concerts or entertainments which the Mozart children gave.

When Wolfgang first gave musical performances, he was so small that he could hardly reach the stool on which to sit, and his legs were so short that his feet didn't always touch the ground!

Probably the grand gentlemen with their powdered wigs and smart shoes with a silver buckle, and the ladies in the gorgeous dresses edged with lace, and their dainty fans, became so curious that they forgot all about their own costumes, and pushed forward in order to get a better view of the 'little magician'.

At that time, there were other kinds of entertainments besides musical ones which were also very popular. Some entertainers owned performing animals; monkeys, for example, who could do all kinds of tricks to amuse people and make them laugh. You might, perhaps, have seen such an entertainer and his pet amusing a crowd of people in the courtyard of an inn, or in a market square.

Other people went to see fights between two cockerels, called cock-fights. This might seem rather cruel to us, today; but in those days the audience became very excited about these fights (no doubt pushing and shoving for a better glimpse of the birds) and they even placed bets on the winner, as people today do at the horse-races.

These cock-fights often used to take place in or near a lane or alley-way. That is why even today you will still see such places called after these events and named Cock Lane, for example.

## Musical activities

1 In the story, Wolfgang is asked to play a tune backwards.
When he grew up, he used a well known tune at the beginning of one of his pieces and then did all kinds of interesting things with it.
Here is the tune, which I expect you have all heard:

It is used as a *nursery rhyme* in this country. Ask your teacher to play it again, and try to say what it is called.

Now clap or tap the rhythm.

Here is the tune again, all through.

How many times can you hear this rhythm?

Now here is the tune played backwards.

Does it sound the same?

6 

2 Here is a tune by Mozart. It is said that he wrote it when he was only six!

Listen once more: here it is again.

Here is the rhythm of this tune:

Clap, or tap this pattern.

This tune comes from a piece called a **minuet**.

Listen to the music all through, and try to find out how many times this first tune is repeated. You will have to listen really carefully all the time.

**Minuet** by Mozart

## Questions to answer

1 How did people travel across the land when Mozart lived? Did they use a car, train, coach and horses or a bus?

2 Look at the pictures of Wolfgang and Nannerl. If *you* were dressed up for a special occasion, would you dress as they did?

3 Wolfgang and his sister were dressed in court costumes to visit the Palace. Do you think that the ordinary boys and girls at that time would have been as richly dressed?

4 It tells you in the story that Maria Antonia (the daughter of the Empress) was called an Arch-Duchess. Her brother was called an Arch-Duke. What do we call the son and daughter of the Queen in *this* country?

5 Every country has a special city which we call the **capital**. What is the capital of these four countries: Austria; England; France and India?

## Things to do

The Mozart family: Father Leopold, Wolfgang, and sister Nannerl.

1 Pretend that you have:

**a** just heard Wolfgang play to a large audience,
*or* **b** just seen a performing monkey,
*or* **c** just watched a cock fight.

Write about what you saw and heard and how you felt.

2 *Either*

**a** Draw or trace the picture of Wolfgang and Nannerl in court costume.

*or*

**b** Draw a picture of the Mozart family journeying to the palace in their smart, hired coach, drawn by four horses. They would be led by a driver handling the reins, perhaps using a whip to spur the horses on.

*or*

**c** Draw a scene from a court ball (or party) for the rich lords and ladies of Vienna. They would be dressed in fine clothes and would be dancing to graceful music in a lovely, large room, lit by many glittering lights.

3 Make up a poster advertising a concert by Mozart. Try to make the poster really colourful, attractive and interesting. If people are curious about someone, they like to find out all they can! For example, you could make people want to know more by heading your poster:
HE IS THE GREATEST!
*or* DON'T MISS THE CHANCE OF A LIFETIME!
*or* COME AND SEE THE WONDER BOY!

**Schubert**

# The Choir School

'Hurry, Franz, it's time for your lesson,' called Papa Schubert. 'Get your violin and come quickly.'

Franz came at once, for he loved music, and didn't mind how much time he spent in learning about it.

'Hold the bow correctly, with your right hand', his father said, 'and rest the violin on your left shoulder. That's coming nicely—well done!'

'When can I have my piano and organ lessons?' Franz asked, eagerly. He was a rather timid, shy boy, and didn't really bother too much about sport or games; but he couldn't wait to learn more about music!

'As soon as possible. We'll try to get you into the Vienna Choir School,' promised Father Schubert.

Although Franz liked to make music and study with his own family—his father and big brothers—he knew that his parents were not rich, and that a scholarship to the famous Imperial Choir School meant that he would receive free lessons and lodging. He also knew that entry to the school would give him many chances to learn much more about singing and playing.

One day, as he was sitting at the piano, his big brother, Ignaz, said, 'Now let's have some sight-reading, Franz. It's very useful to be able to read unknown music quickly and correctly, so that if you meet a singer, you can play the piano part which goes with the song'.

Franz looked at the music which his brother had just placed before him—it was a very pretty song about a violet, by Mozart.

'One day', thought Franz, 'I might even write a song as beautiful as this—and I'll make the piano part sing with the voice part . . . one day . . .'

'Wake up, day dreamer!', cried Ignaz, 'I've got news for

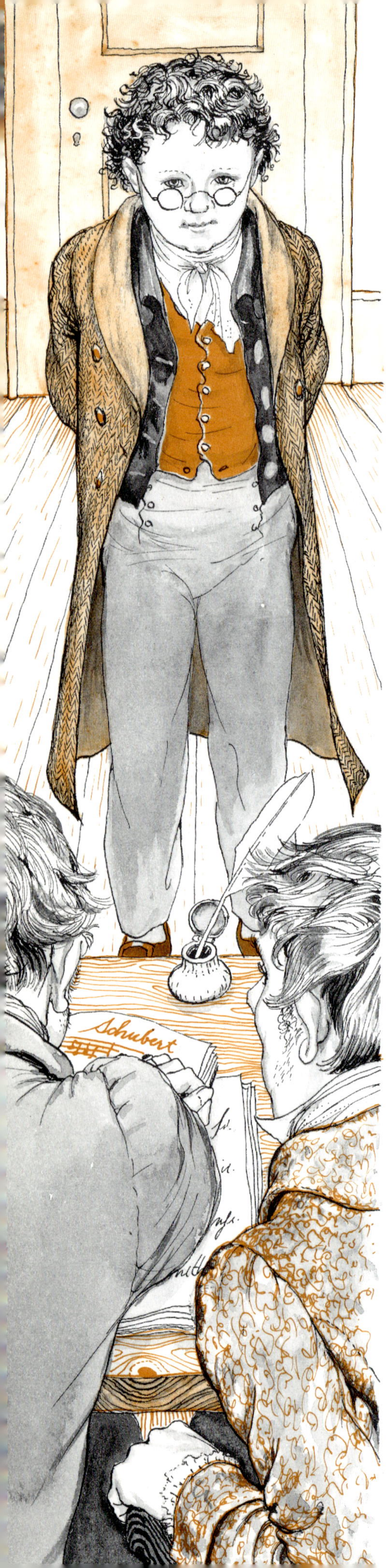


you. Father has said that you are to go for your entrance exam at the music school next week. Just think! You may soon be a choirboy in Vienna!'

A week later, Franz stood—shy and nervous—before his examiners.

'Sing the scale of C,' demanded one stern looking man. Franz's voice went step by step up the notes of the scale: C–D–E–F–G–A–B–C.

'Here is a tune which you have never seen before', he continued, after Franz had finished. 'Look at it carefully, then try to sing it through without a mistake—you'll need to be able to sight read if you come *here*!'

'Now then, my boy', said another examiner, severely, 'what is a crotchet? Look sharp, and answer smartly. We don't want dull-witted lads—we want fine young singers, who are quick to learn.'

Poor Franz! He wanted the floor to swallow him up! But he knew that he must do his best to get into the school; so he went on and on doing as he was asked—singing, playing, and answering questions which seemed to go on for ever and ever!

In time, the verdict was announced, and Franz heard that he was to become a pupil at the Imperial Chapel Choir School. He had passed his tests!

'My!' exclaimed his mother, proudly, 'what grand chances you will have!'

'And all your needs provided for,' added his father.

'You will learn a great deal,' exclaimed his brother, Ferdinand, admiringly.

At last the great day came, and Franz set off from his home in the outskirts of Vienna, to the school in the city. How grand the building looked to the boy from the suburbs!

'Keep well', said his mother, when it was time to say goodbye, 'wash your neck every day, and don't forget your manners'.

'Be a good boy', added his father, 'and learn all you can'.

Before Franz had time to say all the things he wanted to say, he found that his family had left, and that he was all alone—swamped by the big, cold, unfamiliar building.

He was taken to the dormitory which he was to share with other boys, and shown the bed on which he was to sleep.

'You're too late for supper', said the person in charge, 'but breakfast is early, so I expect that you can wait until then'.

Franz was starving and he just didn't know how he was going to get through the long night; but he tried to forget about the empty feeling in his stomach and to think instead about all the music which he might learn the next day.

'I must remember all I know,' he said to himself. 'Now then—*space notes*: F–A–C–E makes "face", *line notes*: E–G–B–D–F makes "Every good boy deserves fun". Let me see—notes of the scale: DOH, RAY, ME, FA'. But before he could go any further, he stifled a yawn, and, tired out by the events of the day, fell asleep.

BOOM! BOOM! BOOM! CLANG! CLANG!

Franz woke up in the cold early morning light, to find the other boys staring at him curiously.

'Hello, tubs!' cried a cheeky-looking boy of about his own age.

'Morning, fatty,' called another, much taller, fair-haired boy.

'What's your name, blinkers?' asked another lad, as Franz (who was really a friendly boy) struggled to keep back the tears which sprang to his eyes at such a rough awakening.

'Franz', he began, shyly, 'Franz Schubert' . . . ('I won't let them see me cry', he thought, 'I'm eleven—I'm too old to cry').

'Fatty Franz! Fatty Franz! . . . Fatty . . .', they all chanted.

But they were interrupted by an older, kind-looking

boy, who said, 'That's enough! Don't be mean! Franz is a new boy—and if you waste any more time, we'll all miss breakfast, and there isn't too much of that, even when we're first at table.'

Franz followed the others to the cold, dimly lit room, where the first meal of the day was served. He was so hungry, and was quite disappointed to see how small his portion was. 'Oh dear!', he murmured, 'I hope my tummy doesn't rumble all through the lessons . . .'

At last the moment he had been waiting for came; he was placed in his position for the choir practice.

'Why, here's old goggle-eyes,' giggled some of his classmates.

'Can you see the music, blinkers?' asked the boy from his dormitory.

Poor Franz! He didn't want to draw attention to himself, so he didn't answer.

But once the practice had started, he got on well; his beautiful voice soared, clearly and sweetly, through the building.

'Well done!' said the choirmaster, turning towards him, and Franz Schubert smiled for the very first time since arriving at the school.

One day, he was sitting all alone in an empty classroom, holding a piece of rather grubby-looking manuscript paper, and singing to himself. In fact, he was so interested in the music which he was composing, that he didn't notice the entry of the kind boy who had stopped the teasing on his very first morning, and had since befriended him.

'That sounds nice,' cried his friend. Franz went scarlet, and put the music behind his back.

'Come on, now, I'm your friend,' reminded the older boy, kindly but firmly. 'Let me see.'

He took the music and began to hum the tune which Franz had written. 'Why it's beautiful! You clever boy!'

Before Franz had time to answer, he said, 'I'll show it to the others', and, without waiting, went across the room calling, 'Hey, you boys, come in here, and listen to the song which Franz has composed'.

The other boys, their curiosity aroused, gathered round, and the older boy sang the melody which Franz had just written.

'Now then', he said, as soon as he'd finished, 'what do you think of *that*? Not bad, eh?'

After that, there was a short, but surprising silence—for a crowd of boys. Then one youngster blurted out, 'Sorry if I teased you, Franz—that song is really good.'

'Yes', agreed another, looking just a little ashamed, 'you really are clever—I couldn't have written that . . .'

'Well done! Well done!' they all cried. Franz felt as though it was the proudest moment of his life! He was really a kindly, sociable boy, not in the habit of bearing ill-will; so he readily forgave the others.

'It's alright,' he said, awkwardly. 'I didn't mind really—well, not always. Anyway, I'm glad—I'm glad you like the song.'

'Three cheers for Franz! And here's a much better nickname—"Songwriter Schubert",' they all cried. 'Three cheers! Three cheers!'

Franz positively beamed with delight behind his glasses! Now it didn't matter about the times when he felt cold and hungry—now he would have other news to write home about besides telling them all that he really did need pocket money for fruit and buns! Now his family could be proud and pleased!

He stood in the cold, bleak room—a short, stocky, bespectacled boy—and suddenly nothing mattered any more except his music.

'When I grow older', he thought, dreamily, 'maybe there will be other songs, even more tuneful and pleasing. One day, I might even be a famous songwriter. You never know, one day the whole world might notice the name of 'Schubert the Songwriter'.

And one day, it all came true! Schubert became one of the most famous songwriters in the world, and a very fine composer.

'Goggle-eyes' really did make good after all!

## Words to remember

**Timid** Not very confident or sure of yourself.

**Severely** Strictly.

**Stern** Stiffly serious; unsmiling.

**Verdict** The answer to something important; a serious decision.

**Soar** To float across the air.

**Bleak** Not at all cheerful or comfortable.

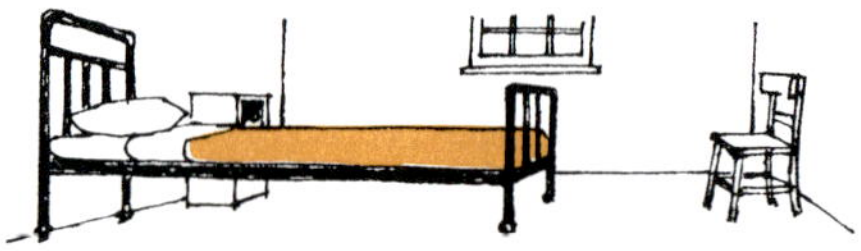

**Curiosity** Really wanting to find out.

**Befriend** To support and make friends with.

## Musical names to remember

**Bow** A kind of stick to which hairs are attached, or joined. It is used by string players to sweep across the strings of their instruments.

**Organ** A large instrument which has keyboards and a row of foot pedals.

**Cradle song** Lullaby; quiet, restful music.

**Melody** The tune of a song; the voice part.

## Things to learn

As you know from the story, Schubert loved to write piano parts which really described the words of the song. He read lots of exciting and colourful poems to get ideas and to spur him on.

One day, he read a poem all about a legend or fairy tale called *The Erl-King*. In this story, during a terrible storm which sweeps across the dark forest, a boy is carried away from his father by the ghastly, ghostly demon, 'the Erl-King'. He cries pitifully for help, and keeps calling 'My father! My father!' But it is no use. The Erl-King has the boy in his clutches and won't let him go. He is lost for ever!

In your *Musical Activities*, you will see a rhythm pattern for the piano part which helps to make the music sound especially 'creepy'.

Schubert wrote music for instruments, as well as for voices, and composed pieces for piano, and for the whole orchestra. Once he wrote a symphony (which is a very important piece for many kinds of instruments) which he didn't finish. So now it is called 'The Unfinished Symphony'.

## Musical activities

7 ♫

**Cradle song** by Schubert

1 Here is a lovely, quiet song by Franz Schubert. It is called *Cradle Song* and it has a beautiful, tuneful melody. Listen to it while it is being played.

This song is in 4 time, which means that it is arranged in groups, or **bars**, of 4, so you would count: 1, 2, 3, 4 | 1, 2, 3, 4 | and so on. Listen to the first group of sounds:

Hum this.
Now sing it.
Now clap it.
Now sing and clap it.

Now listen again to the whole song, and find out how many times this comes. How often is this tune – pattern repeated? Here are the words of this song.

1 *Slumber, slumber, I my watch am keeping,*
*Sleep my baby rock'd by mother's arm;*
*Breezes softly soothe thy sleeping,*
*Gently waft thee far to slumberland.*

2 *Slumber, slumber, here no ill can grieve thee,*
*Sleep my baby sleep on mother's arm;*
*All thy wishes she shall give thee,*
*Rest securely, rest thee free from harm.*

Now sing this song all through. It will help if you remember that the first line of both verses begins: 'Slumber, slumber', and the second line of both verses begins: 'Sleep, my baby'.

Here is a descant recorder arrangement of this song.

You only need these notes to play it:

Look carefully at the recorder part (even if you don't play a recorder!).

You will see signs like this:

These signs are there to tell the recorders *not to play* for a while. Each block—or **rest**—means silence for *four counts*. Musicians in an orchestra sometimes count a group of rests such as these like this:

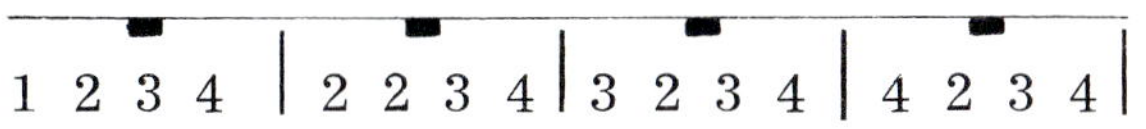


Try to count like that for the recorder players when they come to this part of the song. It should help them to stop—and start again—at the right time! Follow the tune as it is being played.

2 The music which you have just been singing and playing shows how well Schubert makes the piano part suit the tune and words of the song.

Here is a very important sound pattern played by the piano part in one of Schubert's most exciting songs, 'The Erl-King':

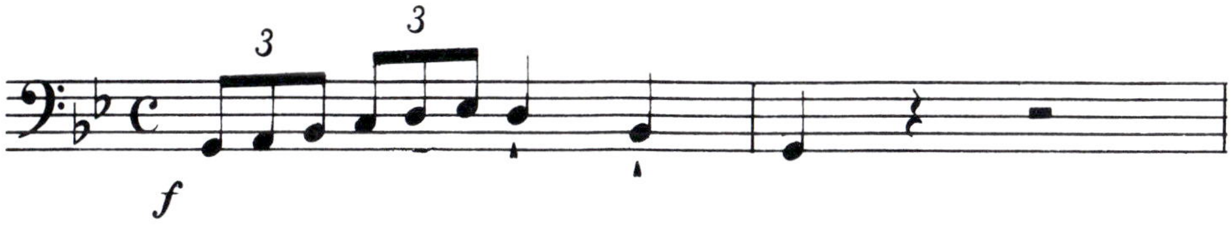

You must admit that it is very 'spooky'!

This sound pattern can be heard many times during the song.

1 Clap this pattern four times.
2 Now find a percussion instrument and play the pattern four times.
3 Now try to make up some frightening and 'spine-chilling' music using that special sound pattern. Imagine that you are in a haunted house, or being chased by an unidentified flying object from outer space!

Get some of your friends to join in with you and add to the ghostly sound effects.

8 ♫

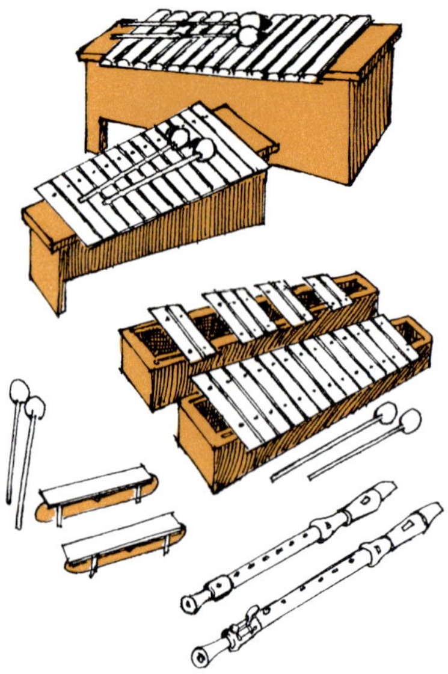

**3** Here is a piece of music by Schubert which would suit percussion instruments. It is called *Ländler*.

If you listen carefully, you will hear that there are some very strong, definite parts, and some light, dainty parts to follow. Try to work out which groups of instruments would suit these two parts. Make your own suggestions. I'm sure that everyone will be glad to listen if you have any good ideas.

When you have finished playing this piece, try—with the help of such instruments as glockenspiel, chime-bars, xylophone, metallophone, recorders—to make up your own tune, or song. Think of some words to suit the music. Perhaps you would like to work in groups, so that each person can add to the effect. Have a go!

**4** Have you ever sung a round, such as 'London's Burning', 'Frère Jacques', or 'Three blind Mice?'

If you have, you will know that it is a song which is split up and sung in groups. You can have as many singing groups as you like. It is rather like a game of musical 'follow my leader', because the group which *begins* (we will call it Group 1) is in the lead, and closely followed by the other groups 2 and 3, and so on.

Here is a round by Schubert. It is called 'O welcome, smiling May'

Listen to this:

**'O welcome smiling May'** by Schubert

Now just sing the last three notes while the tune is played. It will fit in nicely.

This may be rather hard to sing in the same way as the other rounds, but everyone can sing—or play—just the three notes, B–B–E, which come at the end.

## Questions to answer

1 What is a violin bow?
2 What is an organ?
3 What is a scale?
4 Why did Franz Schubert have to take an entrance exam?
5 Name at least *one* of the things which Schubert had to do in order to pass his test for the choir school.
6 What kind of music did Schubert write especially well?
7 What kind of paper do you use for writing music?
8 What was the 'better nickname' which the choir boys gave to Schubert after they heard the song which he had made up?

## Things to do

1 The story tells you about the large, cold rooms of the choir school and how Schubert felt as a 'new boy'. Just think how things have improved today! I expect that you work in a colourful class-room with pictures and charts; perhaps you have a school library and a hall with flowers in it. Write about how *you* felt on your first day at school. Describe what you saw and heard and what you did.
2 In the story, Franz Schubert had to sing a **scale** as part of his entrance exam. A **scale** is a series of eight notes moving up or down in steps. Franz practised the scale—in the way that singers often use it—while in his dormitory.

Here is a diagram which should help you to understand about scales:

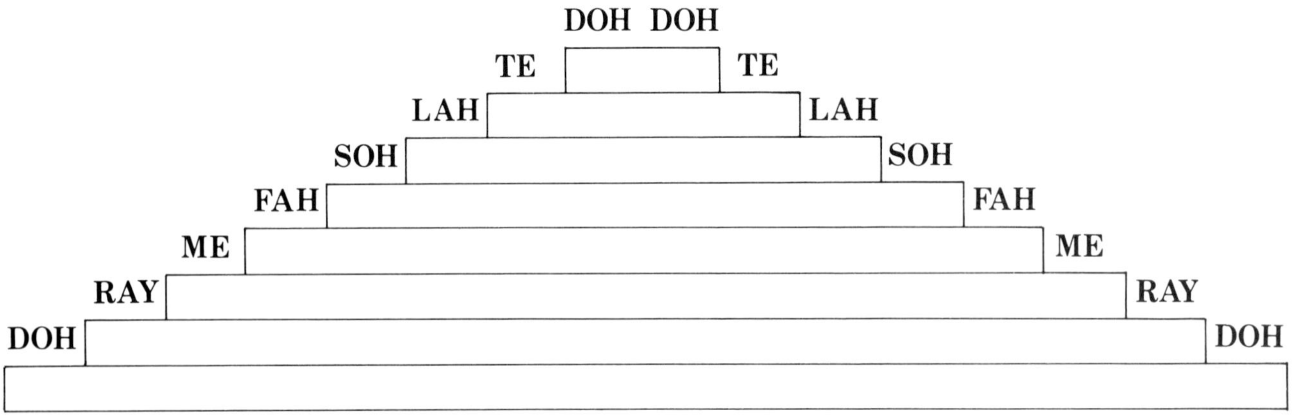


Each step represents a note, or sound.
Copy this diagram and make each row of steps a different shade. *Soh* and *Doh* are very important so give them nice, bright colours!

**3** Here are some German words—and their English meanings—connected with this story:

| **German** | **English** |
|---|---|
| *König* | *King* |
| *Schule* | *School* |
| *Chor* | *Choir* |
| *Musik* | *Music* |
| *Vater* | *Father* |

**a** First, put a piece of paper *over* the English words and see if you can guess what the German words mean—just by looking at them.

**b** Secondly, look very carefully at both lists of words—German *and* English. Then try to work out how many letters are different and how many letters are the same in *each* pair. For example, there is a K in *König* and in King. But which letter comes in *König* but not in King?

If you ever travel to another country on a school journey, or holiday, look carefully at the foreign words, and see if you can work out for yourself what some of these foreign words mean. Have a try!

# The Waltz King

'Schani, Schani', called Frau Strauss, anxiously, 'stop at once! Papa is coming'.

Schani, whose real name was Johann, was standing in front of the long mirror in the Viennese flat which was his home. He was imitating his father (who was a violinist, conductor and composer) and was pretending to be in charge of an orchestra. He was using the bow of his violin as a baton, and was just about to act the part of his father—the great waltz master of Vienna—by conducting a grand waltz (or dance) in front of a huge assembly, when in strutted Father Strauss.

Alas! Johann hadn't stopped in time. Johann Strauss Senior was furious! 'What are you doing with that old fiddle?' asked Herr Strauss. 'I thought I told you to have nothing to do with music! How can you expect to know how to conduct at your age? Music is not for you! Get back to your lessons, boy—*at once*!'

Poor Johann! Before he had time to utter a single word, the instrument was wrenched from his hand and dashed to the ground. He stood still, too dazed to plead, or explain. 'Away with you,' shouted his father. 'Get out of my sight!'

I need hardly tell you that Johann didn't stop to argue—he just fled! 'It's no use,' he murmured, as he crept into bed that night. 'I'll never get Papa to understand. He just won't listen—he won't even give me the chance to explain!'

The next day, however, things didn't seem so bad. Mama was ready to listen, and managed to get him another violin so that he could have secret music lessons with Herr Ammon, his father's assistant. He worked as hard as he could, for he just couldn't wait to become a composer, like his father.

‘How soon will it be before I can become like Papa?’ he asked Herr Ammon, eagerly.

‘Patience, my boy, patience,’ Franz Ammon answered. ‘All in good time.’

‘I hate waiting!’ said Johann. ‘I want to be a musician *now*!’

‘Well, since you’re so keen, I’ll see if I can find you a teacher for composition,’ said the violinist.

‘Make it soon,’ replied Johann. ‘Please!’

In no time at all, Johann was learning how to write music from a Viennese composer. Now, perhaps, Papa would be really pleased with him. Herr Drechsler, his teacher, liked the music which he wrote, so why shouldn’t Papa like it, too?

One day, Johann sat quite still in a corner of the room, listening to his father working. Papa Strauss was composing a polka; but he just couldn’t get the ending to come exactly as he wanted it to do. He had tried several endings, but he wasn’t really satisfied with any of them.

Johann, listening intently, thought of a pretty tune. Why, that would do nicely!

‘Papa, Papa’, he said, ‘let me finish the piece, please! I have a good idea—do listen!’

‘You?’ cried his father scornfully, ‘*you*, Schani! I don’t need any help from *you*!’

Johann turned his face away, angry tears smarting his eyes. ‘Very well’, he muttered defiantly, ‘if Papa won’t listen, then others will. I *am* going to be a composer, come what may! I’ll manage in spite of Papa!’

Johann worked day after day at his music. He didn’t mind, you see, because when he was writing tunes, he was so happy that he forgot all about everything else.

‘One day’, he said to himself, ‘I’ll make all the people in Vienna happy when they hear my music—then maybe even Papa will listen!’

Year after year passed, until at last Johann felt that the time had come to challenge his father. Then it would be *his* turn to show Papa Strauss what he could do!

So he sorted out all the instrumentalists he could find who

didn't have a job, and formed an orchestra. But he couldn't afford a proper hall in which to rehearse, or practise, so he just managed wherever and whenever he could. Worse was to come, for when his father found out what he was doing, he was not just angry, he was absolutely livid!

Strauss Senior got in touch with every single music manager in Vienna. 'If you let my son play in any of the famous ball-rooms, concert-halls, or places of entertainment in Vienna, I'll never play for an audience in these places again,' he roared. 'Do you understand? Never!'

Poor Johann! Papa was still against him! But he didn't give up, which I'm afraid only made his father still more angry—in fact, he was beside himself with rage!

So Strauss Senior got his agent to hire a group of people—rather like football hooligans—to spoil Johann's chances. But it still did not put Johann off—in fact, it only made him more determined than ever!

At last, Johann found a place in which to make his début—at a restaurant called Dommayer's, in a suburb of Vienna outside the main part of the city. He couldn't believe it! His dreams were about to come true. He was going to conduct his own orchestra, playing his own music!

Would people come to listen? Or would they be influenced by his father? If they *did* come, would they like his music? Or would his father manage to spoil everything?

The great night arrived. Johann could hardly wait! He could see row upon row of people, who had come in curiosity to see and hear what Johann Strauss the Second could do. He glanced anxiously at the group of people hired by his father to stop the performance.

'This place is too hot!' they were already beginning to shout, 'and there's no wine to drink—what a dump! I wonder people don't walk out, now!'

Johann turned, and caught his mother's eye. She was sitting at the back of the hall, and smiled at him reassuringly, making him feel more confident. I can't let Mama down, thought Johann—so this is it!

He stood on the rostrum, held up his baton—and began.

For a moment, there was a breathless hush amongst the

audience. Then the hecklers hired by Johann's father started again.

'What a dreadful noise! What a row', they called, 'ugh! I don't call this music! Boo, Boo, BOO!'

But Johann, caught up in his music, didn't even notice! And as the piece came to a grand climax, and reached its peak, making the audience sway to the strains of the swinging dance-rhythm, the sound of the orchestra drowned the noise of the trouble-makers.

They didn't give up, though. They tried hissing, whistling, shouting, banging and stamping. 'Horrible!' they shrieked, at the top of their voices. 'Ugly! DE-TEST-ABLE!'

But nobody was listening to them; the audience was spellbound. All eyes were on the young composer, who looked so handsome in his blue tail-coat, flowered waistcoat, and smart bow-tie.

At the end of each piece, the audience clapped so hard, and the applause was so great, that the trouble-makers were completely drowned! The sounds of 'Again, again! More, more! Encore!' resounded.

In the end, Johann's enemies began to give up, and started to listen, instead of shouting.

'Well,' they thought, 'the boy certainly has talent . . . why, that's rather a nice tune. *Rum*, pum, pum; *Rum*, pum, pum; *Pom*, pom-pom pom; *Pom*, pom-pom pom . . .'

Would you believe it! The hired gang was now listening as eagerly as everyone else!

On and on went Johann's orchestra, playing waltz after waltz, then a polka, called 'Heart's Delight'; and after each item, the audience went mad, and the cheering and applause sounded like the roar of thunder! By now, the people hired by his father were clapping as vigorously and as loudly as the rest of the listeners. In fact, the entire audience could hardly wait for Johann to finish before thunderous applause again and again resounded through the hall.

'Hurray, hurray! Three cheers for Strauss! Cheers for the young maestro! Welcome to the new waltz king! ENCORE!' they all roared.

Do you know, Johann was lifted by two of the men sent by Strauss Senior to upset his performance, who carried him round the hall in triumph! Johann couldn't believe it. At last! He knew that he would never forget this tremendous evening as long as he lived; he was a success.

Tears of joy poured down Mama Strauss's cheeks—her son had made it! She knew—and all Vienna knew—that Johann wasn't just as good as Papa, the Father of the Waltz. Johann Strauss the Second was the new King—the King of the Waltz!

## Words to remember

**Assembly** A large company of people.

**Wrenched** Pulled roughly.

**Assistant** A person helping the man or woman in charge.

**Agent** A person who acts on behalf of an actor, artist or musician.

**Hecklers** People who deliberately interrupt public performances.

**Spellbound** Held as if by a magic spell.

**Triumph** A great success; a victory.

## Musical names to remember

**Waltz** In the time of Strauss, a very popular, gliding ballroom dance in marked three-beat time.

**Polka** A light tripping dance in two-time which was also popular in the days of Strauss.

**Conductor** The person who takes charge of the orchestra and who directs the players with the help of a stick, which he holds in his right hand.

**Baton** The stick used by the conductor to direct his orchestra.

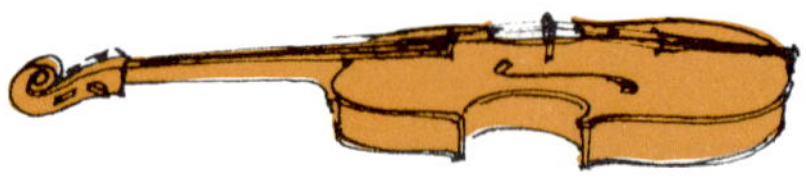

**Fiddle** Another name for a violin.

**Début** To play in public for the first time.

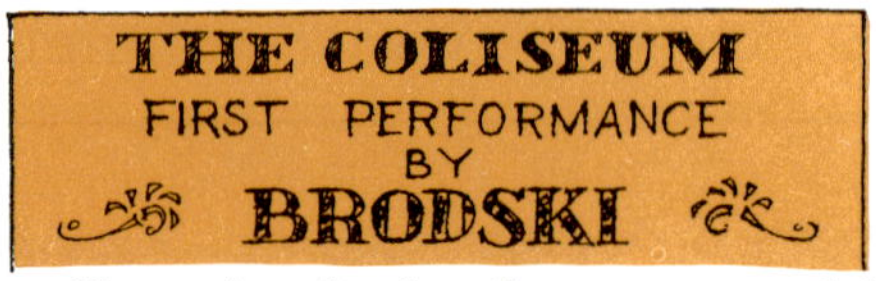


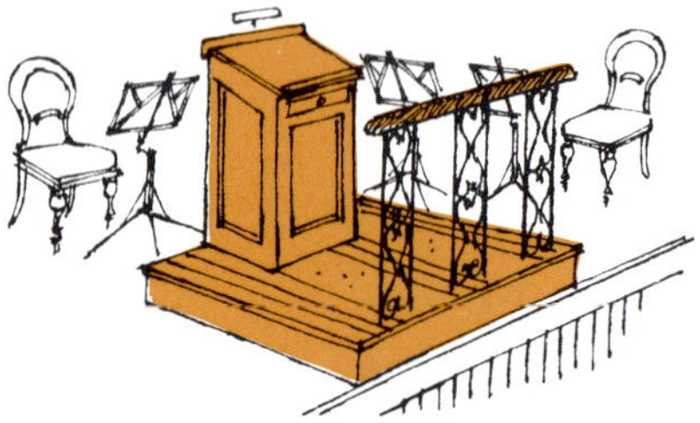

**Rostrum** A small, raised platform, on which the conductor stands so that he can be clearly seen.

## Things to learn

Dancing the waltz at a ball about 100 years ago.

At first, the **Waltz** was a sort of simple, folk dance, which had a lilt, or 'swing': this country dance was then called a *Ländler*. Later, helped by the Strauss family, it grew into the Waltz which was so popular in Vienna and other big cities. Strauss wrote many famous waltzes, and the best known is called the *The Blue Danube*. It is said to be the most popular waltz in the world.

It is easy to clap to the music of this dance, as it goes OOM–cha, cha; OOM–cha, cha. Or: LOUD, soft, soft; LOUD, soft, soft, etc.

Another dance which was very familiar to people in the dance-halls when the Strauss family lived in Vienna, was the **Polka**. This lively dance was a very special one for the ladies because it helped to alter the length of their dresses. You will see if you look at any pictures of ladies who lived before the time of Strauss that they generally wore long, floor-length skirts, and sometimes quite stiff bodices or 'tops.' Well, it would have been very hard for the ladies to dance the quick, light steps of the Polka in dresses such as these! So the skirts of the ladies became shorter (up to the ankle) so that their feet could move freely. No wonder that the Polka is the dance which is said to have changed the ladies fashions! The name Polka means 'half-step', and it is better to clap 1+2+, 1+2+, etc., when you hear this dance.

The famous conductor Sir Thomas Beecham and the London Philharmonic Orchestra. Can you spot the leader?

In the story, Strauss used a **violin** bow as a conductor's baton. The violin is a stringed instrument, and usually the player sweeps the bow across one of the four strings, in order to make the sound. It is a very important instrument in an orchestra, as the leader of the 'violin group' sits at the front, near to the conductor. As he is the best performer in this group, he has to help to keep the other players together, and he is called the 'first violinist,' or 'leader of the orchestra.'

Sometimes, when the composer wants to make a special effect, for example, a crisp, short, sharp sound, the player plucks the strings of his instrument instead of using the bow. This is called **Pizzicato.** Strauss wrote a very attractive polka which shows the effect of plucked strings.

An **Operetta** (a kind of opera) is usually a fairly light-hearted story which is set to music. Strauss wrote some operettas, the most famous of which is called *Die Fledermaus*, which means the 'flying mouse', or bat, in English. This operetta became very popular, as it is very entertaining, colourful and amusing. Most important of all, it has some really pretty, sparkling music.

## Musical activities

1 Here are two dance-tunes which you will enjoy hearing. Ask your teacher if you can clap in time to the music while they are being played.

9 ♫

**'Did you ever see a Lassie?'**

**Ländler** (1) **10**

**Moderato**

**11**

**Ländler** (2)

**2** Here is another folk tune rather like the two which you have just heard and clapped.

Try to play this tune on your descant recorder. It has five notes: B–A–G–low D–top D. Practise finding these notes on your recorder first, and you will find the tune easier to learn!

In a *Ländler* the music is divided into groups of three. The first main tune of the dance you have just heard is made up of these four bars, or groups:

Clap these four bars. How many groups of three have you clapped altogether?

Now listen to the complete dance, again. How many times can you hear the first main tune altogether?

**3** When you have a Music or Activity lesson at school, ask your teacher to play one of the dances from this section. Then, using any percussion instruments such as triangles, woodblocks, tambourines, etc., try to work

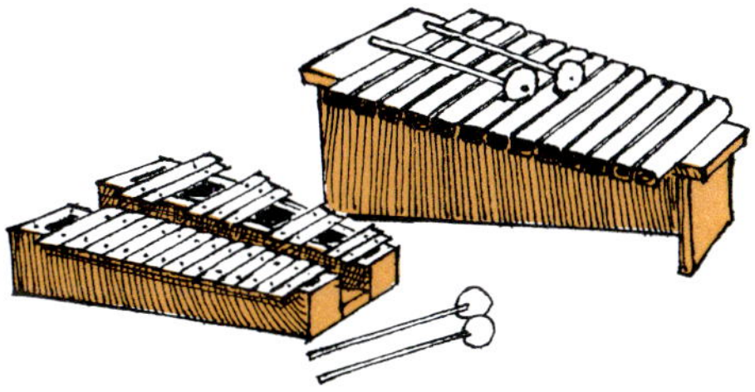

out some instrument groups to play in time with the music. The glockenspiel or xylophone can often help to play the actual tunes.

4 If you have any instruments which can make **chords** (groups of 2, 3 or 4 notes played at the same time and which fit in nicely together) try making up your *own* Ländler.

The recorders or perhaps a stylophone can play a tune taken from the notes GABCD, while such instruments as melodicas, metallophones, small electric organ, or any suitable classroom instrument, can play the OOM–CHA–CHA accompaniment part.

Here is an example of the chords you need to play. Your teacher will show you how to do this. You only need two chords: G chord (G–B–D) and D chord (D–F♯–A).

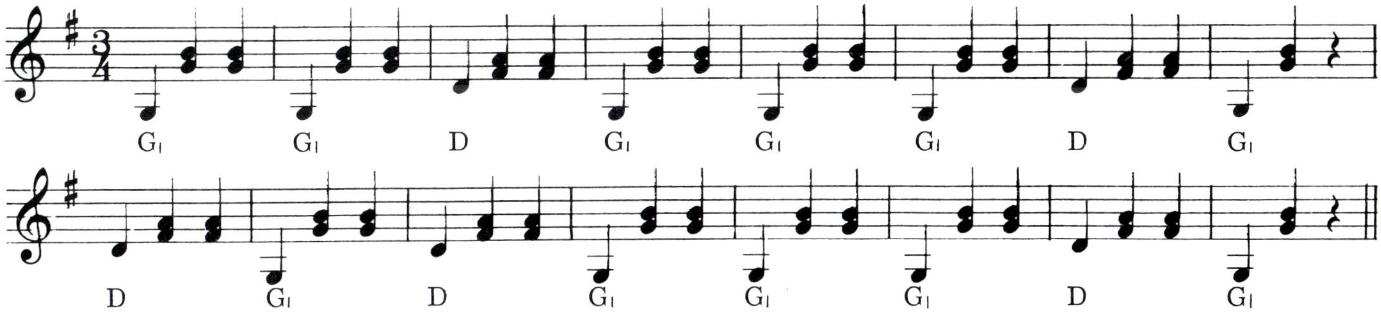


These chords would also fit in well with 'Did you ever see a Lassie?' (page 87), and the third dance in this section which also uses G and D chords.

When you have had enough practice you will be able to work out your own tunes and maybe some chords to go with them. Have fun!

## Questions to answer

1 Who secretly helped the boy Johann Strauss with his musical studies?

2 Who sent the hecklers to try to stop young Johann Strauss's musical début?
3 What is a 'fiddle'?
4 What is a baton?
5 What do we call an early type of waltz?
6 Which dance is said to have changed ladies' fashions?

## Things to do

1 The dances of Strauss are still very popular today. Look in any record shop and try to spot the names of some other famous waltzes, or polkas, by this composer. Make a list of any that you see, and compare notes with your friends. Between you, you should find that you have quite a good list.

2 Pretend that you are young Johann Strauss. You are longing to learn all about music, so you are writing to Herr Franz Ammon, (a musician and violinist in your father's orchestra) to ask—in fact, to *beg*—him to teach you. Remember that the lessons will need to be taken in secret. Your father must *not* know about it!

3 Take the different letters of the name of STRAUSS separately, and use each letter to form the *first* letter of any word connected with music.

*Example*

S *S*ONG
T *T*RIANGLE
R
A
U
S
S

Don't use the two given words—and don't use the *same* word more than once, even though you do have the letter S three times in Strauss's name!

4 Draw a picture of people in Vienna dancing the waltz in a large ballroom, with Strauss conducting.

Grieg

# The boy who didn't like school

'Edward!' called his mother, 'get up, now, please, or you will be late for school.'

'Ugh!' groaned Edward, still half asleep, 'I thought it was Saturday. Three more days to go. How I hate school!' 'SCHOOL!', he muttered, as he put on his shirt, 'Silly old school!' — 'Stupid, stu-pid school', he grumbled, as he put on his trousers. — 'Oh *bother* school!' he cried, as he put on his jacket and he stalked down to breakfast, stamping: 'I HATE SCHOOL! I HATE SCHOOL! I HATE . . .'

'Now then', his mother scolded, 'that kind of behaviour won't get you anywhere. Be a sensible boy, and I will hear your piano pieces tonight.'

'Will you, mother, really and truly?' Edward asked eagerly.

'Yes, if you promise to hurry up and eat your breakfast,' Mrs Grieg answered. 'Come on now'.

Edward felt much more cheerful, and began to enjoy his food.

'Bye bye,' he called to his mother, when he reached the door.

'Goodbye', she replied, 'do try to have a good day'.

Edward felt fine until he was about half way to school, then that old, nasty feeling crept back again.

'Oh dear!' he sighed. 'Teachers! Why can't they let me do my music, instead of those nasty, horrid sums? And why are some of them so grumpy? Why, only the other day they complained—just because I looked at my new piano piece instead of writing on my slate! Grousy old grumblebugs!'

Edward was beginning to drive himself into a really bad, disgruntled mood, and just dragged his feet for the rest of the way.

In the classroom, the same dreary lessons began all over

again. Edward put his head on his hand and leaned on the desk, going through one or two of his favourite piano pieces in his mind.

'Edward Grieg! Edward Grieg!' rapped the schoolmaster, 'Pay attention! Sit up! It will be the cane for you, and a detention after school, if you do not make more effort'.

Edward became very red in the face, but said nothing, as he didn't want to be late home and miss his piano lesson. He wanted his mother to hear the piano music which he was writing.

The next day, it was not just raining—it was absolutely pouring!

'Take care, Edward. Wear your thick boots—and take something to cover your head, too, for goodness sake', his mother added, as she caught sight of Edward running out of home without a cap on.

'Can't—I'll be late,' called that naughty boy, who already had a half-formed plan in his mind.

'Rain! Rain!
Come again!
Never, *never* go to Spain!'

he chanted, jumping into every single puddle, and going under every single wet branch with overhanging, dripping leaves.

On his way to school, Edward passed a rippling stream. He often stopped to listen to the lovely, gurgling, bubbling sound it made, and he was always pleased to see it—but *especially* pleased to-day!

SPLISH! SPLASH! SPLOSH! went Edward's boots, as he waddled like a duck through the brimming stream. Of course, the stepping stones were covered with water; and of course Edward slipped and fell headlong into the stream.

'Wet! *Soaking wet! Whoo!* SATURATED!' he cried out. He trudged on to school and stood before the schoolmaster.

'Excuse me', he began, 'ahem, excuse me, Sir, I'm wet all over'.

'Why, you're *soaked*', replied the teacher. 'What *have* you been doing?'

'Oh dear,' murmured the crafty boy. 'It's such a wet, slithery day—and I have such a long walk to school. I-I fell over into the stream on my way here—I do feel miserable. My mother will worry if she thinks I'm in wet clothes all day.'

'Very well, go home and change into something warm and dry. Off with you, Edward—be back as soon as possible.'

As you can well imagine, Edward had no intention of hurrying. He just took his time, enjoying the countryside in spite of his wet clothes.

By the time he had reached home and found his mother, and told her all about it, and found his dry clothes—well, you can guess what's coming next—it just wasn't worth going back to school. Edward made sure of that!

It had stopped raining by the following morning; and, in any case, Edward couldn't very well get wet again, or find any other excuse for missing school so soon after being sent home.

'Here we go,' he grumbled, as he walked into the school. 'Just when I was beginning to get really interested in making up my music. Botheration!'

Edward wasn't really an awkward boy; so he did try with his lessons in the morning. But by the afternoon, he felt that he just couldn't wait a minute longer to look at the music which he had made up, and to show it to one of his school-friends. So he took the manuscript paper from his bag, and put it under his desk, all ready to show the boy sitting next to him.

His friend whispered to him—hoping, no doubt, that the class teacher wouldn't notice—but of course he did!

'Grieg! Edward Grieg! I spoke to you only the day before yesterday', he bellowed. 'This is too bad—I have had enough! What *do* you two boys think you're doing?'

'Please, sir', started Edward's friend, trying to help, 'Edward doesn't mean to annoy you—you don't understand, sir—you see, he's written some music, he is a compo-'

'He's *what*?' interrupted the teacher.

'Write—writing, er, written—made up some, some music', stammered the other boy.

'Is he, now? Has he, by Jove?', queried the schoolmaster. 'I see, I see! Master Edward thinks he is too clever to bother with his lessons. Master Edward thinks that he doesn't *need* to learn anything besides music—he wants to run before he can walk! DO come here, my young maestro, and show me your masterpiece!'

Edward's cheeks were burning, and his heart was thumping. This time he really was in trouble. He took his crumpled piece of music paper up to the teacher at his desk.

The schoolmaster glanced at it, and hailed the teacher in the next classroom. 'Come! See what my young genius has been doing!'

The other teacher came, and both men studied the music. When the second teacher had returned to his room, Edward looked up hopefully at his own teacher. Perhaps, now, all would be forgiven. But I'm afraid that this teacher didn't really want to know that Edward had made up some really nice sounds. He only knew that the boy should have been concentrating on his lessons.

'Messy!' glared the teacher, looking at the by now rather grubby paper. 'Untidy! SCR-rrr-IB-LED WORK!'. Turning to the class, he went on, 'Sir Edward thinks that he is famous already!' Poor Edward! This teacher wasn't a bit interested in his music, and certainly wasn't going to be very forgiving.

'It's just not good enough . . . away yesterday—misbehaving today', the master continued. 'Be warned boy! If this happens again, you will be in *big trouble*!' And, turning to the cane on his desk, he roared, 'Now get back to your place—my hands are *itching*!'

Edward Grieg moved—like lightning!

At the end of the afternoon, some of his friends gathered around him at the school gates.

'Sorry!' said the boy who had spoken out in his defence.

'Oh never mind', replied Edward, 'I'm not going to give up, you know. I'll write really good music, one day, so that people will like it and won't want to jeer and laugh at me — you'll see!'

And one day he did. Edward grew up to be a very clever composer who wrote piano music and many exciting pieces describing the tales and scenes of his own country.

## Words to remember

**Disgruntled** Cross and resentful.

**Dreary** Boring and uninteresting.

**Headlong** Moving forwards too quickly.

**Queried** Questioned about something which may not be correct.

**Hailed** Called; greeted.

**Influenced** Made to think, feel, or behave in a certain way by others who have an effect upon you.

## Things to learn

Edward Grieg was a very **patriotic** person, which means that he liked and cared about his own country, Norway. In his teens he was sent to study music in Germany; but he later returned, and settled down to compose in Norway. He became friendly with another fellow countryman who was also interested in Norwegian music. In fact, Grieg's friend wanted to develop a

specially Norwegian style of writing music. We call such musicians **national** composers. Grieg was very much affected and influenced by the folk tunes and rhythms of his own people and he was at his best when he portrayed traditional Norwegian music in his pieces.

Once, Grieg was asked to write music based on an old folk legend, or fairy-tale, about a boy called Peter—or 'Peer', in Norwegian. This **Peer Gynt** was a really shocking boy. He was a bully, and was always showing off and causing trouble. He was lazy and good-for-nothing and his poor mother—who wanted him to do well—could only despair of him! In time, he behaved so badly that he had to leave his home and village. He was forced to wander alone through the countryside, which was sometimes wild and craggy. Peer had many exciting and frightening adventures, and he even met the Mountain King and his mischievous dwarfs during his travels. You will learn more about this in *Musical Activities* — so look out for the 'spooky' sounds!

## Musical activities

12 ♫

**In the hall of the Mountain King** by Grieg

1 You have just heard about the story which Grieg set to music. Here is the opening part of the music for one of the pieces from *Peer Gynt*. It describes the hobgoblins or dwarfs, and their leader, or King, and is called *In the Hall of the Mountain King*.

Now try to clap the rhythm pattern as it is being played again.

Here is the pattern yet again, with another musical part joining in with the same rhythm and tune. Perhaps Grieg meant to describe a second group of those creepy little goblins coming in to tease Peer Gynt.

Clap the pattern as it is being played.

Now listen to the next part of this piece. Is this rhythm pattern the same as the one which you have just clapped—or does it change?

If you were listening carefully, all the way through, you may have noticed that the *end* part of the pattern does change—there are not quite as many of the short, quick, running sounds.

If you spotted that for yourself, well done!

Now here is the complete first section of this piece. As you listen, try to imagine how Peer Gynt must have felt when he was surrounded by those weird little creatures.

If you have made any of your own instruments, as suggested, you could use them to play the rhythm pattern, instead of clapping it. Try to get some unusual, unearthly, weird effects!

Finish with a competition.
First, choose any instrument which you like. (Remember that it does not necessarily have to be a percussion instrument. Recorders, for example, can also make some quite startling, wailing sounds, when blown in a certain way.)

Next, sort yourselves out into groups. Keeping mainly to the same rhythm-pattern, work out different sound effects on your chosen instrument.

Then, after you have linked together your joint sound effects, play to each other, to see which group has invented the most frightening effects. Enjoy yourselves!

**13 ♫**

2 Here is another piece by Grieg, called *Grandmother's Minuet.*

As you have already heard, a Minuet is a graceful dance. But because the piece which you are now going to hear was written many years *after* those of Handel or Mozart, it won't sound *exactly* the same as their minuets, although you will be able to hear how well Grieg's music expresses the feeling of this dance. Listen to the first part of it. Now listen again and try to notice this short motive, or little musical shape:

Did you hear it?
Here it is again—but this time, it will sound slightly different, because it is an octave, or eight notes, higher.

Listen again to the first complete section of this minuet, and count how many times you can hear this little musical design altogether.

Now play the whole of this first section, with the piano, using whatever instruments you think would be suitable: drums and cymbals might be too heavy, but triangles and bells would sound very nice. Why not keep one special instrument to play the little design whenever it comes?

14

3 Here is part of another dance by Grieg. It has sometimes been called, or nicknamed *The Grandfather's Dance*, so now you will have heard a piece for Grandmother and a piece for Grandfather!

*The Grandfather's Dance* has become so well known and liked that it has been **orchestrated**, which means that it has been arranged for a group of combined instruments used by an orchestra. While it is being played, try to clap this little rhythm pattern all the way through:

If you can keep this up all the time, then you will be doing very well.
Have a go!

**Grandfather's Dance**
(Norwegian Dance No. 2)
by Grieg

## Questions to answer

1 Where did Edward Grieg live?
2 Who first helped Grieg with his music?
3 Was Edward Grieg's teacher pleased when he discovered that Edward was writing music?
4 Many of Grieg's pieces are about his own country. What do we call a person who writes music of this kind?

5 What is the name of the famous piece which Grieg wrote to describe Peer Gynt's meeting with the Mountain King and his mischievous dwarfs?

6 What is the nickname sometimes given to the last piece (Norwegian Dance No. 2) in the *Musical Activities* section?

## Things to do

The story says that Grieg had a long walk to school. How far do *you* travel to school? Do you walk, or go by bus, train or car?

1 a Find out how far you travel, daily, to and from school, and then work out the distance, or mileage, that you need to cover each week in order to get to—and return from—your school.

b Get each member of the class to write down exactly how they get to school. Then work out how many pupils walk, how many go by public transport (bus, coach, or train) and how many by car. You can then find out which is the most usual way of getting to school.

2 The story describes the running water which Grieg passed during his walk through the countryside to school. What do *you* see on your way to school? Do you pass a bus or a railway station? Do you pass a Post Office, a factory, a library, garage—or another school? Do you pass by any letter-boxes or telephone booths? Do you see a farm, fields, trees or a park? Do *you* see any water—a river, pond, lake, or stream? Do you have to cross any main roads? How many streets do you have to go through before reaching school?

3 a Make a list of all the streets, or roads, which you pass on your way to school. Include any bridges, level-crossings, small lanes or footpaths which you may need to go along if you walk to school.

b Make a list of any useful, important, or interesting buildings or places which you may pass on your way. Do you see any shops, cinemas, or leisure-centres? If you haven't really noticed very much about your journey to school—look on the way home!

4 Grieg did not always like school; and, although it has never been said that he actually ran away, perhaps, when he wanted to finish a piece of music he was composing, he may just have *felt* like playing truant—if only for a day.

During the time when Grieg was a boy, it would not have been possible for him to have gone off to watch aircraft, look at the televisions in the shop windows—or to have telephoned a friend at lunch time, to say how daring he had been! (As you know, in those days, airports and aircraft, T.V. sets and telephones did not exist.)

Imagine that Grieg is a modern boy, just wanting to get away from school for the day. Where would he go? What would he do? How would he travel?

Write about his possible adventures. You could head your story:

'Grieg's day out'

*or* 'A day in the life of a run-away school-boy'

*or* just 'Running away'.

Make your story as lively and interesting as possible. Don't forget to 'wind up' your tale by reaching home by the end of the day—before it is dark!

5 Using the composer's name, GRIEG, take each letter separately, to form the first letter of the name of a country. For example, if you take the composer's name, BACH, and write it as follows, you can form the names of four different countries, beginning with:

B BELGIUM
A AUSTRIA
C CANADA
H HOLLAND

Use a map or an atlas, or a geography book, to help you to find the names of some interesting countries. A globe can also be fun to use!

## Sousa

# The March King

'Prr–rum–pom POM, Prr–rum–pom POM, Prr–rum–pom–pom, rum–pom–pom–POM,' went the drums.

'Taran–ta–TA, Taran–ta–TA,' went the brass instruments.

'Crash–Crash, Crash–CRASH,' went the cymbals.

'Ooh—listen! Listen, Poppa, they're practising next door,' cried John Philip Sousa, excitedly. 'May I join them?'

'Oh, sure', laughed his father, who was himself a trombone player in the Marine Band, 'when you are old enough'.

'Oh, gee!' wailed John Philip, 'I can't wait till I'm grown up—that's years and years and years . . .'

'Never mind', interrupted John's mother. 'Practise your music for at least an hour every day, and that will make the time pass more quickly. Then, when you are a man, think how well you will play!'

'When I'm older! When I'm a man!That's all the grown-ups ever say—wait, wait, wait!' muttered John, as he opened the door; but, instead of going to practise, he stole into the nearby barracks, imitating the military musicians as he strode along. Up went his hands when copying the brass players. Down, up, left, right, went his arms, when imitating the drummers. In his own mind, John Philip wasn't just one of the band players: he was the *leader* of the band!

In fact, he was so keen, that, not long afterwards, he decided to start his own group in the neighbourhood. Anyone who could manage to play a suitable military band instrument could join; and soon, John's band was doing remarkably well—so well that it drew quite a lot of local attention.

One day, as John was strolling near his home, he saw a procession of carts, horse-drawn caravans, ponies, monkeys, a chimpanzee—and, yes, there it was—a real, live elephant!

John couldn't wait to get home to tell his parents.

'Gee, Momma, guess what?' he called, bubbling over with excitement. 'The circus is coming—may I go to see it?'

'Calm down,' laughed his mother. 'Give the circus people time to settle in—they won't be ready to start performances today if they are only just arriving.'

'When shall I go, then?' asked John, eagerly, 'tomorrow?'

'As soon as they are open, I promise you,' replied his mother.

At last it was time for John to visit the circus; and he wondered happily which turn, or event, he would like most. Would it be the pretty girls balancing on the ponies' backs? Would it be the daring trapeze artists? Or would it be the lions he had heard roaring in the distance? No, perhaps, after all, it might be the circus music—John was really looking forward to the bright, lively, stirring sounds which he was about to hear.

'Hello, young fellow-me-lad', a man's voice called, as John Philip approached the circus grounds, 'aren't you the boy musician I've heard about—the young band master?'

John flushed till his face was scarlet. 'Er, yes, as a matter of fact, I am,' he answered.

'Well, now, what do you know!' the circus leader continued. 'I do declare you're just the very chap I've been looking for! How would you like to come and work for me?'

'For—for you?' John asked, excitedly. 'Do—do you mean as a musician? *Me?*'

'Sure—I think you could make the grade,' replied the circus leader.

'Gee!' was all John could find to say; and then, after a pause—'WOW!'

'Well?' questioned the man.

'Of course I'll come', said John. 'I'll join you tomorrow—'

Although John enjoyed the circus, he couldn't wait to get home to start packing. You see, he had already planned

exactly what he was going to do. He knew that his father would not allow him to become a circus musician; so he had decided to run away. He thought about what he would need: some clothes, his whistle, the small knife which he had been given might be useful—and, of course, he mustn't forget his music!

He walked into his home with a mysterious air.

'Well?' began his mother. 'Tell me all about it.'

'Oh—yes', replied John; and then, unexpectedly, he went on, 'I'll tell you later, Momma—I—I've got to go right now'.

'Well!' exclaimed his mother. 'I am surprised! Why, you've been just fretting to get to that circus ever since it arrived; and now that you've seen it, you've hardly got time to talk about it —'

But John Philip had not even waited for his mother to finish speaking!

All that evening strange sounds and peculiar noises could be heard from John's bedroom, as he went about the business of packing. He was so thrilled about the circus offer that he didn't stop to think whether his parents might hear down below.

'What *is* going on up there?' enquired John's father, later that night.

'Goodness knows!' answered his mother. 'He's been acting strangely ever since he got back from that circus.'

'Has he, now?' mused his father. 'Well, we'll see about that.'

Up the stairs went Mr Sousa, to find John hastily shoving

a package under the bed as his father entered the room. Mr Sousa looked round, and said, 'Why, you've packed all your music! Whatever for?'

John went red. 'Oh, just for fun—I mean, I might be going to play to the boys, tomorrow,' he added, lamely.

'Well, now . . .', was all his father said, in a slow, pondering way. 'Really!'

Mr Sousa went back to talk to his wife, who said, 'John's so mad about that darned circus—you don't think—he *can't* be planning to . . . ?'

'To run away?' finished Mr Sousa, 'yes it's possible—but you can bet your bottom dollar, he isn't going to!'

Dawn came, bringing the first early morning light. The great moment had arrived for John Philip, who crept out of his room stealthily and nervously. He mustn't wake a soul! He was holding his belongings, and there was nothing on his feet, so why did the stupid floor creak when he was walking?

'Never mind,' he thought. 'A few more steps—just a few steps more —'

Soon, he would be out of the house. Before very long, he would be moving on with the circus. He just couldn't imagine how thrilling it would be —

'And where do you think *you're* going, young man?' asked John's father, as he put a firm hand on John Philip's shoulder.

'Let me be, please,' cried John. 'I've got to go—you don't understand what a chance I'll be missing if I don't. I'm going to be the leader of the circus musicians. You MUST let me go!'

'Never!' answered his father. 'Understand this: you don't set foot outside that door without my permission. Now take yourself back to bed where you belong—there is no more to be said'.

'Please', cried John, 'Dad! PLEASE!'

'No,' said Mr Sousa.

'Very well, then', answered John, 'I won't practise ever again, not for you, or Momma, or anyone else; and, what's more, I'll never try to make up another march tune as long as I live—never ever!'

So saying, John stamped upstairs, seething with angry disappointment at the thought of his lost chance.

And that, you might think, was that.

But it wasn't, for you'll be pleased to know that Mr Sousa didn't want to discourage John or spoil his son's chances—he just wanted his musical activities to be sensible; so he very soon arranged for John to become an apprentice, or pupil, in the Marine Band, instead of becoming a circus musician. It wasn't long before John forgot all about the circus job; and he did very well during his eight years' apprenticeship.

John Philip really did become a band leader, and his band travelled far and wide, and became very famous under John's direction. In fact, his marches gained so much applause and he made up so many fine, rousing tunes for his instrumentalists to perform, that he became known throughout the world as the one and only 'March King'.

## Words to remember

**Military** Connected with soldiers or armed forces defending the country in time of war.

**Stealthily** Secretly careful and quiet.

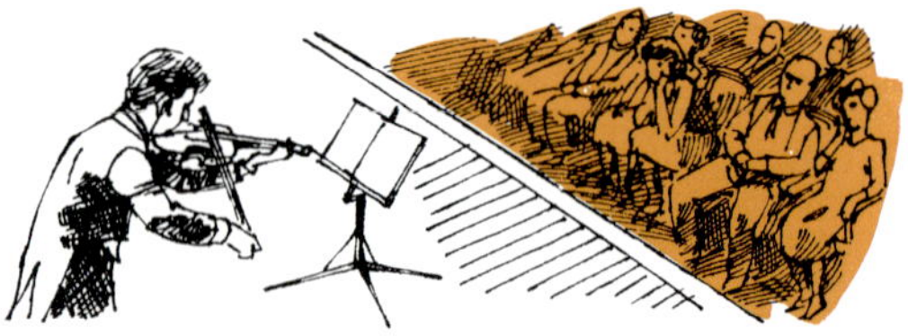

**Perform** To play music—often in public—to a high standard.

## Musical names to remember

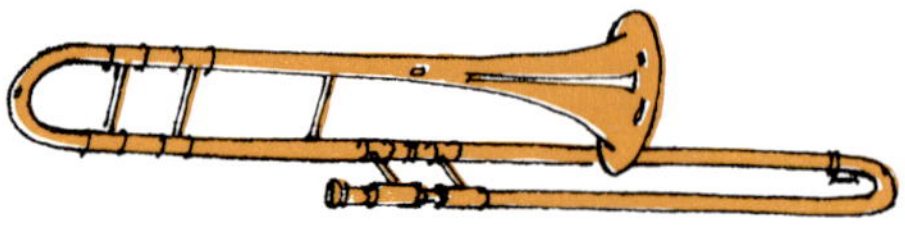

**Trombone** A brass instrument which has a slide moved in and out by the player to control the sounds.

**Sousaphone** A huge brass instrument which curls round the player's body and is played in bands.

One of Sousa's marches, *Liberty Bell* , was written to commemorate the Statue of Liberty which overlooks New York harbour.

## Things to learn

As you heard in the story, Sousa became America's most famous composer of band music. Some of his best loved marches were written for special occasions. *The Washington Post March* was written for the prize-giving of a Public School's Essay Competition, sponsored by *The Washington Post. The High School Cadets' March* was written for the cadets parading in Washington. The march which Sousa composed in connection with a world tour was called *Hands across the Sea*.

Sousa's most popular march, *Stars and Stripes Forever*, takes its name from the stars and stripes which can be seen on the American flag. When Sousa was returning from a tour, he stood on the deck of the steam ship; and a fine, stirring tune came into his head. He heard the whole band playing in his mind; and he imagined the music so clearly and vividly that he was able to write the whole march down on paper as soon as he reached America. This piece is still performed by bands all over the world on many different occasions — when astronauts land, for example.

Sousa's band was so popular and successful, and the effects which he created were so stirring, that a brass instrument was named after him, and was called the **sousaphone**.

## Musical activities

1 Listen to this short tune, or musical sentence:

Now listen to it once more. Here it is again:

15

This tune comes from a rousing march by Sousa, called *The Belle of Chicago*. Here is the first part of this march. Listen carefully to find out how many times you can hear this particular tune.

**The Belle of Chicago**
by Sousa

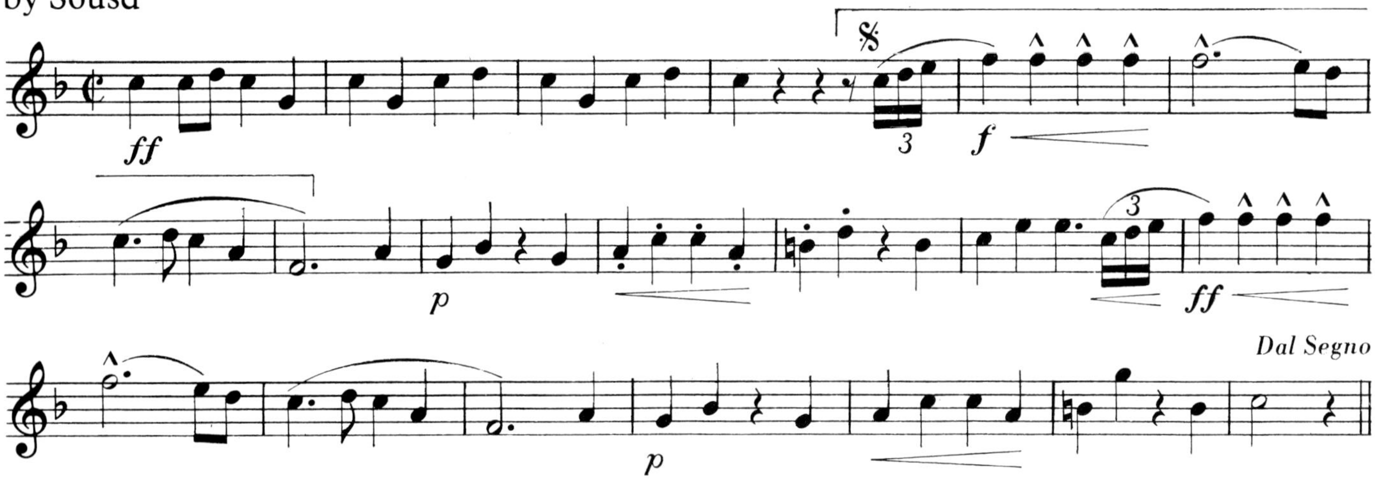


16

2 Here is a rhythm pattern. Listen to it:

Now listen to it again. Then clap, or tap, the pattern, while it is being played for the third time.

Here is the pattern again. It comes from a march by Sousa called *Liberty Bell*. How many times can you hear exactly the same pattern?

**Liberty Bell**
by Sousa

Now here is the second part of this march.
While you are listening, try to work out which percussion instrument you would like to use when you play this piece yourself.
Remember that some of the instruments which you often play, such as the drums and cymbals, would have been used by Sousa's band musicians.

Now play both parts of this march as a complete piece. Pretend that you are a member of a famous band!

3 Make up a march of your own. Here are some of the rhythms which your drummers could beat:

a 

b 

c 

Don't forget to use your cymbals; but don't use them all the time, or you will drown everyone else. Just let them play on the special clashes. Strong, marked beats in music are sometimes shown by a short line just under or above the note. If you look at your drum-beat rhythms carefully, you will find some of these lines, called **accents**.

## Questions to answer

1 What is the name of Sousa's most famous march?
2 Name three other famous marches written by Sousa.
3 Read the first part of the story carefully, then say why you think that John Philip first became interested in the music of the Marine Band.
4 Why was John Philip so excited after going to the circus? Why did he decide to run away from home?
5 How did Sousa's band become well known?
6 What was Sousa's nickname?
7 Which instrument was named after Sousa?

## Things to do

1 In the story, Sousa went to the circus.
*Either*
a Think about the time when *you* went to the circus. Describe some of the turns, or events, which you most enjoyed, such as the clowns, or lions, etc. (If you have never visited a circus, or watched one on television, you could always write about an *imaginary* visit, and describe the things which you would most *like* to see!) You could head your work 'My visit to the circus'.
*or*
b Pretend that you are a young 'run-away' circus musician. Write about your life with the circus people; your caravan home; your travels; and the excitement of a first-night performance in a new town.
You could head your work 'Life at the circus'.
*or*
c Pretend that you are a circus clown. Sometimes it is great fun to put on a silly 'make-up' face, turn somersaults, and make everyone laugh; but, when you feel sad about something, it is quite hard to be jolly and funny all night.

How do you think that you would *really* feel when you are tripped up, or when someone throws a wet, sticky, custard pie in your face?!
You could simply head your work 'I am a clown'.

**d** You have heard about some of the places where lively, rousing march music can be heard: at a circus, on parade, or at a public event such as a prize-giving. Make a list of any other special occasions when you might expect to hear Sousa's marches being played — at a football match, or when astronauts land, for example.

2 Make a list of all the animals which you would be likely to see at a circus. Then, with the help of an animal or wildlife book, or perhaps a junior dictionary, write by each animal the country to which it belongs.
*Example* Elephant — Africa or India.

**3** Find a map and try to trace a possible journey by Sousa from Washington to the continent of Europe. Which is the most direct sea route, and which is the nearest European country on which the ship might land?

**4** In *Things to learn*, you read that Sousa's famous march *Stars and Stripes Forever* was named after the American flag. Look in a travel book, a book about flags and banners, or perhaps a Junior Encyclopaedia. When you have found the American flag; trace, or draw, and colour it. If it is a small-sized illustration in the book, some of you might like to make a larger one — it could look very colourful.

5 Draw *either*

**a** A scene or picture of a circus event: ponies, trapeze artists, for example.

*or*

**b** A clown, with perhaps a red button nose, orange eyes, and green hair. Have fun!

**6** With some paints, scissors, scrap materials and card or some other strong paper, make your own ideal hat for a clown to wear. Enjoy yourselves!

# Music quiz

You will need to look through different stories in this series to help you to find some of these answers.

## Jumbled names

Sort out the following to make the name of a composer:

**1** CABH
**2** DLEHNA
**3** ZOMRTA
**4** STSUARS
**5** TBCHUSRE

## Missing words

Put in the missing letters to finish these sentences:

**6** STRAUSS lived in V_____.
**7** GRIEG lived in N_____.
**8** MOZART travelled throughout different countries in E_____.
**9** In VIENNA there is a RIVER called the D_____.
**10** BACH lived in G______.

## Opposites

A piece of music can be:

**11** Soft or ________
**12** Long or ________
**13** Slow or ________
**14** High or ________
**15** Happy or ________

**Back to front**

Here are the names of some of the pieces mentioned in this series. Put these titles in the right order:

16 KING ERL THE
17 DANUBE BLUE THE
18 STAR LITTLE TWINKLE TWINKLE
19 SYMPHONY SURPRISE THE
20 FOREVER STRIPES AND STARS

**'Odd one out'**

Re-write these groups of linking words. Each time, leave out the word which does not fit in with the others in the group:

21 WALTZ, POLKA, MARCH, MINUET.
22 CLAVICHORD, HARPSICHORD, PIANO, BANJO.
23 SILK, TAFFETA, LACE, COACH, CLOTH.
24 PRINCESS, EMPRESS, KING, COMPOSER, QUEEN.
25 MELODY, TUNE, SONG, HYMN, SYMPHONY.

# Piano arrangements

## 1 Musette – Bach

## 2 Symphony No. 94 'Surprise' – Haydn (Arr. T.M.)

## 3 **Country Dance** – Haydn

## 4 **Symphony No. 104 'London'** (Last movement) – Haydn (Arr. T.M.)

## 5 **Austrian Hymn** – Haydn

GLORIOUS things of thee are spoken,
  Sion, city of our God!
He whose word cannot be broken
  Formed thee for his own abode:
On the Rock of Ages founded,
  What can shake thy sure repose?
With salvation's walls surrounded,
  Thou may'st smile at all thy foes.

J. NEWTON, 1725–1807

## 6 **Minuet** – Mozart

# 7 Cradle Song – Schubert

# 8 Ländler – Schubert

## 9 Did you ever see a lassie? – Traditional (Arr. T.M.)

Tempo di Valse

## 10 **Ländler** (Country dance) (1) – Traditional

## 11 **Ländler** (Country dance) (2) – Traditional (Arr. T.M.)

## 12 **In the hall of the Mountain King** – Grieg (Abridged)

## 13 Grandmother's Minuet Op. 68 No. 2 – Grieg

## 14 Grandfather's Dance (Norwegian Dance) Op. 35 No. 2 – Grieg (Simplified)

## 15 **The Belle of Chicago** – Sousa (Arr. T.M.)

## 16 **Liberty Bell** – Sousa (Arr. T.M.)

# Music to use

All records and music listed below are reasonably priced and available at the time of publication. The suggested piano pieces are well within the range of the average piano player.

Each record and book contains several items directly relating to the musical work on a particular composer, thus ensuring that the teachers get material that is not only educationally useful but also good value for money.

## Handel

**Records**

Suite No. 1: Water Music
Suite No. 2: Music for the Royal Fireworks DSLO595

*Alternatively:*
Water Music Suite, Music for the Royal Fireworks
Hallelujah Chorus from *Messiah*
The Arrival of the Queen of Sheba (DSLO594)
All on D242D3

**Piano music**

Gavotte *Classics to Moderns Series No. 2*
Rigaudon *Classics to Moderns Series No. 3* (Yorktown Music Press Inc. dist. Music Sales, 78 Newman Street, London W.1)
Minuet in F *Pleasure in Progress* (Associated Board, 14 Bedford Square, London W.C.1.)
March from *Scipio* and March 'See the conquering hero comes' from *Judas Maccabaeus* *Twelve Famous Marches* (Cramer, 99 St. Martin's Lane, London W.C.2.)

**Piano and recorder arrangements**

*Handel Album for recorder and piano* arr. for descant and/or treble and tenor recorders by Walter Bergmann (Schott, 48 Great Marlborough Street, London W.1.)
Includes Air (from *Water Music*), Minuet (from *Berenice*), Gavotte, Pifa (Christmas Pastorale from *Messiah*), March, Minuet (from *Fireworks Music*), Tamburino, Bourrée and La Réjouissance (from *Fireworks Music*).
*Second Handel Album* arr. Bergmann (Schott)
Includes 'See the conquering hero comes', Musette (from the masque *Terpsichore*), Caro, Alla Hornpipe, Minuet in D major (from *Water Music*)

## Bach

**Records**

Orchestral Suite in D major (No. 3 *Gavotte,* No. 4 *Bourrée,* No. 5 *Gigue*)
A number of recordings readily available.
The Brandenburg Concertos (6747166)

Sheep may safely graze (ASD14 36421)

**Piano music**

Musette and March from *The Notebook of Anna Magdelena Bach*
Musette from Gavotte and Musette (English Suite No. 6) *The Joy of Bach* (Yorktown Music Press Inc. dist. Music Sales)
*Other pieces by Bach's relatives:*
Johann Christoph Friedrich Bach Country Dance, English Dance, Peasant Dance
Carl Philipp Emanuel Bach Andantino Cantabile, Solfeggio
Wilhelm Friedrich Bach Variations on a French Song (Twinkle, twinkle, little star)
Wilhelm Friedrich Ernst Bach Two Waltzes
Little Prelude *Classics to Moderns Series No. 3* (Yorktown Music Press Inc. dist. Music Sales)

## Haydn

**Records**

*Excerpts from the following symphonies (all of which are readily available on record):*
Symphony No. 101 in D major ('Clock') Slow movement
Symphony No. 100 in G major ('Military') 2nd and last movements
Symphony No. 104 in D major ('London') Last movement
Symphony No. 94 in G major ('Surprise') 2nd movement
The 'Toy' Symphony (DG 2531275)
The 'Farewell' Symphony (slow movement)

**Piano music**

*Second Year Haydn* arr. E. Markham Lee (Lengnick and Co. Ltd.)
Includes Minuet (from the 'Toy' Symphony), Canzonetta 'My mother bids me bind my hair', St Anthony Chorale, German Dance.
Little Serenade *Classics to Moderns Series No. 2* (Yorktown Music Press)
Schäferlied *Pleasure in Progress* (Associated Board)
The Clock on the Wall Op. 62, No. 3 (Kullak) *Pleasure in Progress* (Associated Board)

## Mozart

**Records**

Overture to *The Marriage of Figaro* *Favourite Overtures* (Contour CC 7531) Serenade No. 13 (*Eine Kleine Nachtmusik*) Symphony No. 40 March in C, K408
All on CC7507

**Piano music**

*First year Mozart* arr. R. Kreutzlin (Lengnick and Co. Ltd. Purley Oaks Studios, Brighton Road, South Croydon)

Includes Theme and Three Variations in C on a French Melody (Twinkle, twinkle, little star), Introduction, Scherzino, Classic Waltz, Ländler

Minuet and Spring Song *Classics to Moderns Series No. 2* (Yorktown Music Press)

Air from *The Magic Flute* *Progressive Pieces* (Elementary Grade) (Associated Board)

March from *The Marriage of Figaro* *Twelve Famous Marches* arr. Carol Medway (Cramer)

A Musical Joke (Sextet in F, K.522) *T.V. and Film Classics* (EMI Ltd.)

(Horse of the year show theme suitable for piano or electric organ)

Ländler *The Joy of Recital Time* (Yorktown Music Press)

## Schubert

**Records**

Overture to *Rosamunde*, The Magic Harp *Favourite Overtures* (Contour Red Label CC7531)

*Rosamunde* Entracte 2 (ASD14 36421)

The Erl King (SXLP30553)

**Piano music**

Waltz *Classics to Moderns Series No. 3* (Yorktown Music Press)

Various pieces from *First year Schubert/Second year Schubert* (Lengnick & Co. Ltd.)

Valse sentimentale from *The Joy of Romantic Piano* (Book 1 — Early to Intermediate Grades) (Yorktown Music Press)

Marche Militaire from *It's Easy to Play Marches* arr. Cyril Walters (Wise publications)

## Grieg

**Records**

Peer Gynt Suite (various recordings)

Peer Gynt and Wedding Day at Troldhaugen (DGG 2535635)

Holberg Suite (ASD14 36421)

**Piano music**

*Grieg: An introduction to his piano works* (ed. Margery Halford) (Alfred Publishing Co. Ltd.) (Contains the full version of *Grandmother's Minuet,* and various other suitable items including Waltz, Gjendine's Lullaby Op. 66, No. 19, Sailor's Song Op. 68, No. 1, A tune from Siri Dale.)

Norwegian Dance *Classics to Modern Series No. 3* (Yorktown Music Press)

Various pieces from *First year Grieg/Second year Grieg* (Alfred Lengnick & Co. Ltd.)

'Morning' from Peer Gynt Suite *Themes from T.V. and Film Classics* (EMI Ltd.) Suitable for any kind of electric keyboard or piano.

## Strauss

**Records**

Waltzes from *Tales from the Vienna Woods* (JB 68)

*Strauss Waltzes* London Philharmonic (CFP 165),

SDD 133 (Fiori Collection) and GL 43706 (Ace of Diamonds) include:

The Blue Danube, Artist's Life, Roses from the South, Emperor Waltz, Wine, Women and Song, Accelerations Waltz, and the Pizzicato Polka by Johann and Josef Strauss

Radetsky March (Available on *Marschmusik*—see Sousa)

Overture to *Die Fledermaus* *Favourite Overtures* (CC 7531)

'You and you' and other excerpts from *Die Fledermaus* (2532025)

**Piano music**

The Blue Danube, The Emperor Waltz, *It's Easy to Play Waltzes* arr. Cyril Walters (Wise Publications)

Radetzky March *It's Easy to Play Marches* (Wise Publications)

Radetzky March *Twelve Famous Marches* arr. Carol Medway (Cramer)

Artist's Life *T.V. and Film Classics* arr. Cecil Bolton and Jack Moore (EMI Ltd.)

## Sousa

**Records**

12 marches in *Sousa the March King* Band of the Royal Corps of Transport (DR 17) Includes 'Hands across the Sea'. Complete with pictorial record cover showing the American flag, instrument and picture of Sousa.

The Washington Post march orch. Sousa, Stars and Stripes forever, Semper Fidelis, El Capitan March *The Military Band* (SM 1056 Capitol)

Washington Post March plus various marches and other Sousa compositions *Marschmusik* Ariola 201443 241/401443 242

**Piano music**

Washington Post, Stars and Stripes forever, Liberty Bell *It's Easy to Play Marches* (Wise publications)

Liberty Bell *Twelve Famous Marches* arr. Carol Medway (Cramer)